AirPorts

AirPorts

J·S·K

Dipl. Ing. Architekten

Zweite Auflage | *Second edition* (2003)

© 2001 Ernst Wasmuth Verlag Tübingen · Berlin
Lektorat | *Copy editors*:
Sigrid Hauser, Ursula Kleefisch-Jobst
Titel- und Buchgestaltung | *Cover- and book design*:
Rosa Wagner
Herstellung | *Production*:
Rosa Wagner
Übersetzung ins Englische | *Translation into English*:
Janet Brümmer BA, Düsseldorf
Reproduktionen | *Artwork*:
Druckhaus Cramer, Greven
Druck und Bindung | *Printed and bound by*:
Druckhaus Cramer, Greven
Printed in Germany

ISBN 3 8030 0618 X

Die Deutsche Bibliothek – CIP Einheitsaufnahme

Ein Titeldatensatz für diese Publikation ist
bei Der Deutschen Bibliothek erhältlich.

6

Die Entwicklung der Flughäfen reflektiert weltweit die sich verändernde wirtschaftliche, gesellschaftliche und industrielle Entwicklung seit Beginn des Siegeszugs der intelligenten Technologien. Flughäfen haben mit der Entwicklung des Massenflugverkehrs Quantensprünge vollzogen. Gebäudetypen sind entstanden, deren Wachstum ungebrochen erscheinen und die der Entwicklung von Städten und Regionen ihren Stempel aufprägen. Vom einstigen Solitär vor den Grenzen der Städte hat sich der Flughafen zum Tor der Stadt selbst und zum Motor ganzer Regionen entwickelt.

Bedingt durch das stürmische Wachstum im Flugverkehr mußte die Architektur neue Wege finden. Die Planungen neuer Flughäfen, insbesondere der Großflughäfen, folgen der Architektur aus einem Guß. Die komplexen Logistikanforderungen sind in einfachen, identitässtiftenden Großformen wie zum Beispiel der großen Halle organisiert, der architektonische Bezug zur Region wird hergestellt, und der ökologischen Sensibilität wird Rechnung getragen.

Den Rollenwandel des Airports in der postmodernen Großstadt hat der Architekturtheoretiker Deyan Sudjic wie folgt umschrieben: „Der Flughafen übernimmt zunehmend die Funktion des mittelalterlichen Marktplatzes". Er ist das Zentrum, das von der Bevölkerung einer Region jährlich mehrfach aufgesucht wird. Flughäfen sind kleine Städte mit Dutzenden von Läden, gastronomischen Betrieben, mit Bahnhöfen, Konferenzzentren, Kinos, Bürobauten, Hotels, Banken und anderen Einrichtungen geworden.

Vor dem Hintergrund dieser sich abzeichnenden Entwicklung und der dabei in Deutschland zu erwartenden herausgehobenen Position der Stadt Frankfurt am Main habe ich 1963 in der Mainmetropole ein eigenes Architekturbüro gegründet. Die hausintern durchgeführten städteplanerischen Analysen, die daraus abgeleiteten Prognosen für die Mobilität und Flexibilität der Menschen erbrachten als Ergebnis, daß weltweit ein erhöhter Bedarf an Airports zuzüglich der dazugehörenden Infrastrukturen entstehen würde. Es erschloß sich damit ein neuer Markt, der zugleich den Anbau zusätzlicher Kompetenzen und Know-hows in meinem Büro erforderte.

Mit dem ersten Großauftrag in diesem Bereich, dem Bau des Sheraton-Hotels am Frankfurter Rhein-Main-Flughafen, ist auch die Geburtsstunde des Architekturbüros J•S•K verbunden. Ich ging eine Partnerschaft mit den Braunschweiger Architekten Reinhart W. Schulze und Karsten Krüger-Heyden ein.

Dieses Hotel hatte Signalwirkung auf die weitere Entwicklung an Rhein-Main. Der Trend zum Airport als Kommunikationszentrum setzte sich ungebremst fort. Mit dem Bau des Frankfurt Airport Center (FAC) schuf J•S•K für den Flughafen Einrichtungen, welche dessen Drehscheibenfunktion voll und ganz aufnahmen. Der Flughafen wurde zum Treffpunkt einer globalisierten Gesellschaft.

Die rasant gestiegene Zahl der Flugbewegungen sowie der Passagiere war mit dem Terminal 1 nicht mehr zu bedienen, so daß sich die damalige Flughafen AG – heute Fraport AG – entschloß, ein weiteres Terminal zu bauen. Mit diesem Auftrag eröffnete sich J•S•K 1988 ein neues Kapitel der Unternehmensgeschichte. Der Ausbau der Drehscheibenfunktion und der Erhalt der Wettbewerbsfähigkeit zwangen den zweitgrößten Flughafen Europas dazu, zu expandieren und großvolumig zu investieren. Mit dem Terminal 2 mußte ein Abfertigungsgebäude mit einer Struktur geschaffen werden, die alle Prozesse am Boden optimal abbilden läßt, eingebettet in eine Architektur, die Transparenz und Übersichtlichkeit für den Fluggast wie für die Mitarbeiterinnen und Mitarbeiter ausstrahlt. So erhielt das Terminal eine lichte Check-In-Halle in leichter Stahl-Glas-Konstruktion, mit der die extremen Spannweiten überbrückt wurden. Ein People-Mover-System verbindet die beiden Terminals.

J•S•K hat mit seinem Entwurf die Stahlbau-Architektur des Frankfurter Hauptbahnhofs als Beispiel genommen und sie mit modernen Werkstoffen umgesetzt. Beide erfüllen die Funktion, „Tor zur Stadt" zu sein.

Es gehört zur Unternehmenskultur von J•S•K, nicht nur mit kreativen und machbaren Entwürfen aufzuwarten, sondern sich auch durch Kunden- und Servicenähe auszuzeichnen, dort zu sein, wo der Kunde ist. So wurde 1987 – an einem für uns strategisch wichtigen Standort – ein weiteres Architekturbüro in Düsseldorf eröffnet, das von Jurek Slapa, Zbigniew Pszczulny, Helmut Oberholz, Jonas Jacobitz, Wolfgang Marcour und mir geleitet wird. Von dort aus planten und realisierten wir die Erweiterung des Flughafens Münster-Osnabrück, an dem jährlich bis zu zehn Millionen Passagiere abgefertigt werden können.

Nach der schrecklichen Brandkatastrophe am Flughafen Düsseldorf im Jahre 1996 stellte sich J•S•K einer erneuten Herausforderung: der Sanierung und Erweiterung des Airports in der nordrhein-westfälischen Landeshauptstadt. Aus dem hierfür ausgeschriebenen internationalen Wettbewerb ging J•S•K mit seinem Beitrag als Sieger hervor, der ein ausgewogenes Verhältnis zwischen innovativen Konzepten und praxisbewußter Realisierung ist. Die Jury lobte unseren Entwurf als „ein homogenes Gesamtbauwerk ohne Bruch in der gestalterischen Aussage". Der Neubau erfolgte während des laufenden Flugbetriebs. Es war, wie der Kunde sagte, „eine Operation am offenen Herzen", die erfolgreich verlief.

Nach dem Fall der Mauer und der Wiedervereinigung Deutschlands expandierte J•S•K weiter. Seit 1991 entwickelt und steuert das Unternehmen in von einem von Gunter Bürk, William Joslin, Michael Stutz, Florian Beck, Volker Rumler und mir in Berlin gegründeten Büro die Aktivitäten in der neuen Hauptstadt und ihrem mittelbaren wie unmittelbaren Einzugsgebiet. Auf Grund unserer vielfältigen Kompetenzen im Flughafenbau sind wir mit mehreren Planungen für den Bau eines Berliner Großflughafens an die Öffentlichkeit getreten. Den neuen Flughafen Berlin-Brandenburg bearbeitet J•S•K in einer Arbeitsgemeinschaft mit gmp.

Bereits in den 80er Jahren entwickelte J•S•K Studien, um die verschiedenen Verkehrsmittel und -wege zusammenzuführen. Die Verbindung von Schiene, Luft, Straße und – möglicherweise auch – von Wasserstraßen gehört zu den modernen Verkehrskonzepten der Zukunft und erhöht die Mobilität der Menschen ebenso wie die Transportmöglichkeiten von Frachtgütern.

Mit „AiRail" ist am Flughafen Rhein-Main europaweit eine innovative und richtungsweisende Lösung gefunden worden, die Pilotfunktion hat. J•S•K ist nach einem internationalen Investoren-Architekten-Wettbewerb beauftragt, die Knotenpunkte Flughafen, ICE-Bahnhof sowie Autobahnkreuz auf intelligente Weise in einer Form so zu verknüpfen, daß sie über die Verkehrsnutzung hinaus Dienstleistungsfunktionen übernehmen können. So entsteht über dem dem Flughafen Rhein-Main vorgelagerten ICE-Bahnhof ein ca. 800 Meter langes gläsernes Gebäude, in das Hotels, Bürogebäude, Shopping-Bereiche und die Bahnhofshalle integriert werden.

J•S•K hat in mehr als 30 Jahren die Kompetenz in der Planung und im Bau von Flughäfen erworben. Wir rekrutieren uns aus qualifizierten Partnern, Teamleitern, Mitarbeiterinnen und Mitarbeitern, die bereit sind, mit uns immer wieder neue Wege zu gehen, neue Ideen zu kreieren, dabei aber nie den Blick für das Machbare zu verlieren. Wir setzen auf die Erfahrung unserer älteren Mitarbeiterinnen und Mitarbeiter genauso wie auf die Visionen, mit denen die Jüngeren unsere Arbeit begleiten. Uns allen liegt eines am Herzen: Der Transfer der vielfältigen Anforderungen und der technischen Abläufe eines Flughafens in ein attraktives Gebäude.

J•S•K arbeitet aktuell an den Airports:
    Fraport, Frankfurt am Main
    airport 2000 plus, Düsseldorf
    Flughafen Berlin-Brandenburg International, Berlin
    Flughafen Frankfurt-Hahn
    Airbase Ramstein
    Flughafen Warschau
    Flughafen Zürich-Kloten

Meinen Partnern und dem ganzen J•S•K-Team danke ich für viele Jahre vertrauensvoller und erfolgreicher Zusammenarbeit. Sie haben dabei mitgewirkt, daß wir uns national und international zu einem kleinen Kreis von Architekturbüros entwickelt haben, die einen Airport professionell planen und betreuen können – bis hin zu dem Gesamtkomplex des Airports als „Kern einer neuen Stadt".

Mein besonderer Dank gilt meinem Partner Karsten Krüger-Heyden, der dieses Buch konzeptionell entwickelt und wesentliche Passagen geschrieben hat.

Helmut W. Joos, Dipl. Ing. Architekt
Seniorpartner von J•S•K

Frankfurt am Main, im November 2001

The ongoing restructuring and expansion of airports is a reflection of the worldwide changes in economic, social and industrial development since intelligent technologies began to advance. With the constant increase of mass air transportation, airports have also been growing in leaps and bounds. We now have building types that seem to expand endlessly and which have a noticeable impact on the development of cities and surrounding regions. Once lonesome riders banned to the outer limits of cities, airports have now become the gateways of these cities and also transportation hubs for entire regions.

Determined by the rapid growth of air transport, architecture has had to forge new paths as well. The planning of new airports, in particular major international airports, goes hand in hand with architecture. Complex logistics demands are organised in large simple buildings with unmistakable identities, such as main terminals with their spacious concourse areas; the architectonic relationship to the region is established and ecological aspects are also taken into consideration.

The changing role of the airport in the post-modern metropolis has been described by architecture theorist Deyan Sudjic this way: "The airport is increasingly taking on the function of the medieval marketplace". It is a central pivot point that is visited by the population of a region many times each year. Today's airports have become mini-cities with dozens of shops, restaurants and snack bars, railway stations, conference centres, cinemas, office complexes, hotels, banks and a host of other facilities.

In view of the developments taking place and the consequences that these changes would have for the city of Frankfurt/Main in Germany, I founded my own firm of architects in the Main metropolis in 1963. The city planning analyses that we carried out and the resulting forecasts for the mobility and flexibility of people were translated into a worldwide higher demand for airports and their accompanying infrastructures. This brought with it a new market, which at the same time meant the necessity for additional spheres of competence and know-how in my offices.

Our first major project in this field, the construction of the Sheraton Hotel at Frankfurt Airport, was closely connected to the birth of the J•S•K firm of architects. I entered into a partnership with two architects from Braunschweig, Reinhart W. Schulze and Karsten Krüger-Heyden.

The hotel triggered further development projects at Frankfurt Airport. The trend towards the airport as a communications centre continued unimpeded. With the construction of the Frankfurt Airport Centre (FAC), J•S•K created facilities for the airport that supported its transport hub function in every way. The airport became an important meeting point for a global society.

However, the rapidly increasing number of flights and passengers soon became too much for Terminal 1 to handle alone, so Fraport AG – then called Flughafen AG – decided to build a second terminal. With this project in 1988, J•S•K entered into a new chapter of entrepreneurial history. The expansion of air transport and the need to maintain a leading position in the international market made it necessary for the second-largest airport in Europe to expand and make major investments. The new Terminal 2 was to become a passenger handling centre with a structure that would optimally facilitate all processes on the ground, imbedded in an architecture characterised by transparency and clarity for easy orientation not only for passengers but also for airport staff. Therefore the terminal was designed with a light and airy check-in hall spanned by a wide steel and glass construction. A People Mover system connects the two terminals.

J•S•K based its concept on the steel architecture of the main railway station in Frankfurt and implemented the plans with modern materials. Both of these fulfil the function of a "city gateway".

An integral part of the company philosophy at J•S•K, besides offering creative and feasible drafts for projects, also includes being close to the customer to provide the best possible service. Therefore, in 1987 we opened an additional office of architects in Düsseldorf – a location that was strategically very important for us – to be managed by Jurek Slapa, Zbigniew Pszczulny, Helmut Oberholz, Jonas Jacobitz, Wolfgang Marcour and myself. From there we planned and realised the expansion of the Münster-Osnabrück airport, with an annual handling capacity of up to ten million passengers.

After the terrible fire at Düsseldorf International Airport in the year 1996, J•S•K faced another new challenge: the rebuilding and expansion of the airport in the capital of North-Rhine Westphalia. The international competition for this project was won by the concept submitted by J•S•K, which is a well-balanced combination of innovative concepts and practice-oriented realisation. The jury praised our design as "a homogeneous construction with a consistent creative statement". The building measures took place during normal airport operations. It was, as the customer phrased it, like doing "open-heart surgery", but work progressed smoothly and successfully.

After the Berlin wall came down and Germany was reunified, J•S•K expanded further. Since 1991, in an office opened by Gunter Bürk, William Joslin, Michael Stutz, Florian Beck, Volker Rumler and myself in Berlin, the company develops and runs activities in the new capital and its direct and indirect hinterland. Thanks to our wide diversity of expertise in the field of airport construction, we have gone public with several concepts for the construction of a major Berlin Airport. The new Berlin-Brandenburg airport is being developed by J•S•K in collaboration with gmp.

As early as the 1980s J•S•K carried out studies that linked the various transport systems together. The connecting of rail, air and road traffic – and even river transportation – is among the modern transportation concepts of the future: it increases the mobility of people and also improves the transport of freight goods.

With the "AiRail" station at Frankfurt Airport an innovative and trend-setting trans-European solution with a pioneering function was created. Based on a design concept that won the international investor and architectural competition, J•S•K had the task of finding an intelligent solution for linking the airport, the ICE station and the motorway junction, to create a combined system to efficiently accommodate services as well as regular traffic. The result was a glass building, approx. 800 metres long, built in front of the ICE railway station at Frankfurt Airport, in which hotels, office complex, shopping arcades and the railway station are integrated.

J•S•K has acquired a wealth of expertise in over 30 years of planning and building airports. We recruit qualified partners, team leaders and staff who are all willing to forge new paths with us again and again, and to create new ideas without ever losing sight of the feasible. We count on the experience of our senior staff members just as much as the visions and ideas brought in by our junior team members. We share one top priority – the transfer of diversified requirements and technical processes of an airport into an attractive and functional building.

J•S•K is currently working on the following airports:
Fraport, Frankfurt / Main
airport 2000 plus, Düsseldorf
Berlin-Brandenburg International, Berlin
Frankfurt-Hahn Airport
Ramstein Airbase
Warsaw Airport
Zurich-Kloten Airport
I would like to thank my partners and the entire J•S•K

team for many years of loyal and successful collaboration. They are the reason why we can count ourselves among the small circle of national and international firms of architects that are able to professionally plan and manage the development of an airport – including the entire complex of the airport as the "core of a new city".

My special thanks go to my partner Karsten Krüger-Heyden, who developed the concept for this book and wrote major parts of the text.

Helmut W. Joos, Dipl. Ing. Architekt
senior partner of J•S•K

Frankfurt/Main, in November 2001

Unsere Welt und unsere Zivilisation sind ohne Fliegen und ohne Flughäfen nicht mehr denkbar. Die Entwicklung des Flugverkehrs hat lange vor der Verbreitung der neuen Medien dazu beigetragen, daß dieser Globus kleiner wurde und Entfernungen sich verkürzten. Die Welt hat auch durch das Fliegen an Gleichzeitigkeit des Geschehens gewonnen. Diese Entwicklung wird sich trotz des Terrorakts vom 11. September 2001 auch weiter fortsetzen.

Flughäfen heute sind technische, wirtschaftliche und städtebauliche Zentren ersten Ranges. Die ehemals kleinen und eindimensionalen 'Luftstützpunkte' haben sich zu riesigen Verkehrsknotenpunkten, aber auch zu großen Warenhäusern und Marktplätzen entwickelt. Neben dem An- und Abfliegen können hier auch alle anderen Bedürfnisse befriedigt werden, die der moderne Mensch für wichtig hält und braucht, vom Shopping jeder Art bis zum Kinoerlebnis, vom Kunstgenuß bis zur Fitneß, vom Tagen und Konferieren bis zum gepflegten Essen.

Neue Flughäfen sind Städte eigener Art, und sie werden wie neue Städte geplant. In den großen Ballungszentren dieser Welt, vor allem in Südostasien, haben sie auch die Größe von städtischen Gebilden. Man kann neue Flughäfen heute durchaus mit den Idealstädten der Renaissance vergleichen, insofern sie aus einem Guß geplant sind. Während die Idealstädte aber fast ausschließlich Planungen auf dem Papier blieben, werden Flughäfen heute allerorts gebaut. Und ein Ende des derzeitigen Flughafenbooms ist nicht abzusehen.

Flughäfen sind komplexe technische Maschinen. Die Fülle ihrer Funktionen macht sie zu faszinierenden Gebilden. Diese technischen Gebilde sind gleichzeitig gigantische Architekturaufgaben. Auch in einer Zeit zunehmender Globalisierungstendenzen bleiben Flughäfen deshalb die Visitenkarten eines Landes und das jeweilige Tor zur Welt. Das bedeutet, daß sie bei aller funktionalen Einheitlichkeit individuelle regionale Bauaufgaben sind. Der ankommende und abfliegende Mensch möchte wenigstens an einigen Eigenarten erkennen, wo er sich gerade befindet.

Die schönsten Flughäfen sind die, welche nicht nur reibungslos funktionieren, sondern auch als Stadt und Architektur beeindrucken: in der Organisation, in der Atmosphäre, in der gestalterischen Anmutung.

Prof. Dr. Ingeborg Flagge
Direktorin
Deutsches Architektur Museum

Frankfurt, im November 2001

Our world and our civilisation are impossible to imagine without flying and air traffic. Long before the advance of the new media, the development of air transportation was already playing a major role in making our planet smaller and distances shorter. Flying has also increased the simultaneity of events in our world. And this development will also continue despite the terrorist attacks of 11 September 2001.

Today's airports are first-class technical and economical centres of urban development. What were once small one-dimensional 'air bases' have since become huge transport hubs, large warehouses and international marketplaces. In addition to aircraft take-offs and landings, a host of other needs can be fulfilled here – needs that are important for modern people, from every kind of shopping, going to the cinema, enjoying art and staying fit, to meetings and conferences and even fine dining.

New airports are cities in their own right and they are therefore planned like cities. In the major overcrowded areas of the world, in particular South Asia, they are also the same size as cities. New airports can easily be compared with the ideal cities of the Renaissance in that they are planned as a homogeneous unit. But while those ideal cities almost exclusively remained unrealised concepts on paper, today airports are being built all over the world. And no end to the current airport boom appears to be in sight.

Airports are complex technical machines. The scope of their functions makes them fascinating structures. These technical creations are at the same time gigantic architectural challenges. Even in this day and age of increasing globalisation, airports remain the calling card of a country and its gateway to the rest of the world. This means that they are, with all their functional units, individual construction projects specific to the region in which they are built. Arriving and departing passengers want to see at least some sign of where they are in the world. The most beautiful airports are those which not only run smoothly, but are also impressive as a city and in terms of their architecture: in their organisation, in their atmosphere and in their creative ambience.

Prof. Dr. Ingeborg Flagge
Director
German Museum of Architecture

Frankfurt, in November 2001

In diesem zweiten Buch über J•S•K Architekten fokussieren die Verfasser auf deren Arbeiten an Flughäfen, eine architektonische Besonderheit bzw. Herausforderung an Gestaltung, Funktionalität, Wirtschaftlichkeit und nicht zuletzt Ästhetik.

Das Wirken und der Grundstein des Erfolgs des Architekten Helmut Willy Joos gehen auf das Gründungsjahr seines Büros im Jahre 1963 in Frankfurt zurück. Mit der ersten Bauaufgabe am Frankfurter Flughafen, dem Sheraton-Hotel, ging er eine Partnerschaft mit Reinhart W. Schulze, Braunschweig, ein. 1980 wurde von den Architekten Helmut W. Joos, Reinhart W. Schulze und Karsten Krüger-Heyden das Büro J•S•K Dipl. Ing. Architekten in Frankfurt am Main gegründet.

Das Sheraton-Hotel war in den 70er Jahren des letzten Jahrhunderts das erste Gebäude, welches am und um den Flughafen Frankfurt am Main von den Architekten Helmut W. Joos und Reinhart W. Schulze geplant und später von J•S•K in zwei Ausbaustufen erweitert wurde.

Es folgten weitere Projekte dort, wie z. B. das FAC-Frankfurt Airport Center, die Brücken zwischen Terminal 1, dem Hotel und FAC, ein Schulungszentrum sowie ein Teil der Cargo City Süd, Werkstätten und ein Casino sowie einige dazu gehörende Planungen, die nicht realisiert wurden.

1968 erhielt J•S•K den Auftrag für das Terminal 2, wobei die Planungen zunächst vorsahen, das Parken in drei Parkgeschossen auf dem Terminal stattfinden zu lassen. Das Konzept wurde vom Flughafen geändert, und die Stellplätze wurden in einer Tiefgarage vor dem Terminal untergebracht, das eine lichte attraktive Check-In-Halle erhielt – mit einem People-Mover-Bahnhof, der die beiden Terminals verbindet.

Am Terminal 2 sind die Grundsätze der Gestaltung von J•S•K gut abzulesen. Die Transparenz in der Funktion und der Gestalt steht im Vordergrund ihres Schaffens, um dem Menschen die Architektur nutzbar zu machen. Er ist das Maß, das jeden Entwicklungsprozeß bestimmt. Die Flughäfen mit ihren vielfältigen Ansprüchen und Funktionen erfordern für den Nutzer Klarheit, sinnfällige Orientierung und eine einfache, verständliche Abfolge von Funktionen – das, was die Architekten von J•S•K als „Transparenz" bezeichnen, wobei damit auch dem ästhetischen Empfinden Rechnung getragen wird.

1987 wurde in Düsseldorf ein weiteres J•S•K-Büro gegründet, das von den Architekten H. W. Joos, J. Slapa, Z. Pszczulny und H. Oberholz geleitet wird. Dem Frankfurter Terminal 2 folgten nationale und internationale Flughafen-Wettbewerbe im In- und Ausland, ab 1987 auch die Erweiterung des Flughafens Münster-Osnabrück für bis zu 10 Millionen Passagiere pro Jahr. International waren J•S•K Architekten z. B. tätig und erfolgreich, als sie für HOCHTIEF die Planung des neuen Flughafens Athen Eleftherios Venizelos abwickelten.

Nach dem tragischen Brand des Flughafens Düsseldorf gewann das Unternehmen 1996 mit einem sehr attraktiven Konzept den internationalen Wettbewerb. Im laufenden Jahr sind denn auch die Terminals A, B und C mit dem ersten Teilstück der gekrümmtem zentralen Halle in Betrieb gegangen.

1991 gründeten die Architekten Helmut W. Joos und Gunter Bürk, William Joslin, Michael Stutz, Florian Beck und Volker Rumler ein weiteres Büro in Berlin. In über zehn Jahren wurden mehrere Planungen für den neuen Berliner Flughafen entwickelt. Den neuen Flughafen Berlin-Brandenburg bearbeitet J•S•K nunmehr mit gmp in einer Arbeitsgemeinschaft.

Vor dem Flughafen Frankfurt am Main plant J•S•K nach einem internationalen Investoren-Architekten-Wettbewerb ein sehr interessantes zukunftsweisendes Projekt, das Schiene, Luft und Straße miteinander verbinden wird. Über dem ICE-Bahnhof vor dem Flughafen wird ein ca. 800 Meter langes gläsernes Gebäude entstehen, das den beziehungsreichen Namen „AiRaiL" trägt. Als Einrichtungen sind über die Verkehrsnutzung hinaus Hotels, Büros und ein Health-Care-Zentrum vorgesehen. In der Haupterschließungsebene, die eine verglaste Dachkonstruktion erhält, werden die einzelnen Eingangsbereiche der Facilities in einen interessanten Shopping-Bereich eingebettet.

Alle Flughafenplanungen, ob realisiert oder nicht, zeigen die große Erfahrung und das breite Spektrum der Architekten von J•S•K bei der Bewältigung der Aufgabe, die vielfältigen Anforderungen und die technischen Abläufe eines Flughafens in ein attraktives funktionstüchtiges Gebäude zu übersetzen. Dabei müssen viele Disziplinen des Flughafens geordnet, miteinander verknüpft und mit der Architektur in Einklang gebracht werden. Im Mittelpunkt aller Überlegungen steht der Mensch als Nutzer des Flughafens. Die Wirtschaftlichkeit der Planung und die Kosten sind ein weiterer Schwerpunkt. J•S•K ist eines der wenigen Büros, die nicht nur einen Flughafen planen können, sondern ihn auch über die Objektüberwachung bei der Realisierung begleiten.

Jeder Flughafen stellt neue Anforderungen. Immer wieder sind Kreativität, Innovation und der Sachverstand der Architekten von J•S•K von neuem gefordert. Sie zeichnet besonders aus, daß sich unter ihren vielen nationalen und internationalen Flughafenprojekten drei große deutsche Flughäfen befinden, bei denen J•S•K hervorragende Fachkompetenz für die professionelle Flughafenplanung unter Beweis stellt.

Dr.-Ing. Götz Herberg
Vorsitzender der Geschäftsführung der
Berlin-Brandenburg Flughafen Holding GmbH
Flughafen Berlin-Schönefeld

Berlin, im November 2001

In this second book about the J•S•K firm of architects the author focuses on the work that J•S•K has done on airports, and the special architectonic features and challenges that are involved in terms of design, functionality, economics and, not least, aesthetics.

The fundament of the success enjoyed by architect Helmut Willy Joos can be traced back to 1963, the year he founded his company in Frankfurt. With the first development project on the Sheraton Hotel at Frankfurt Airport, he formed a partnership with Reinhart W. Schulze from Braunschweig. In 1980 J•S•K Dipl. Ing. Architekten was founded in Frankfurt/Main by architects Helmut W. Joos, Reinhart W. Schulze and Karsten Krüger-Heyden.

In the 1970s of the last century, the Sheraton Hotel was the first building in the Frankfurt area to be planned by architects Helmut W. Joos and Reinhart W. Schulze and later developed by J•S•K in two phases of construction.

Further projects followed this, for example the Frankfurt Airport Centre (FAC), the bridges between Terminal 1, the hotel and the FAC, a training centre as well as a section of Cargo City Süd, workshops and a casino and also several concepts for further development that were not realised.

In 1968 J•S•K was given the Terminal 2 project, the plans for which initially included three park decks on the roof of the terminal. However, the concept was altered by the airport and instead an underground parking garage was built in front of the terminal, which was given an attractive check-in hall – with a People Mover connecting the two terminals.

The basic design principles of the J•S•K architects can clearly be seen in Terminal 2. Transparency in both the function and the design stands on centre stage of their creation, resulting in architecture that is not only a pleasant atmosphere but also a functional building for people to use. Transparency is the standard on which every development process is based. Airports with their wide diversity of needs and functions demand clarity, easy orientation and a simple concept that is easy for the user to see and understand – which is what the architects at J•S•K call "transparency", and which fulfils an aesthetic function as well.

In 1987 a second J•S•K office was opened in Düsseldorf, which was managed by architects H. W. Joos, J. Slapa, Z. Pszczulny and H. Oberholz. Terminal 2 of Frankfurt Airport was followed by national and international airport competitions, both in Germany and abroad. The expansion of the Münster-Osnabrück airport to accommodate up to 10 million passengers per year was commenced in 1987. In the international arena the J•S•K architects were also successful with a concept they developed for HOCHTIEF for the new Athen Eleftherios Venizelos airport.

After the tragic fire in Düsseldorf International Airport the company won the international architectural competition in 1996 with a very attractive design concept. In the year 2001 Terminals A, B and C and the first section of the curved central concourse were opened for business.

In 1991 a further office was opened in Berlin by architects Helmut W. Joos and Gunter Bürk, William Joslin, Michael Stutz, Florian Beck and Volker Rumler. Over the course of the next ten years numerous concepts for the new Berlin Airport were developed. The new Berlin-Brandenburg airport was designed by J•S•K in collaboration with gmp in a working coop.

Based on a design concept that won an international investor and architectural competition, J•S•K is now building an extremely future-oriented project in front of Frankfurt Airport, which will connect air, rail and road transportation systems. Over the ICE railway station in front of the airport a glass building, approx. 800 metres long, is being built, bearing the significant name "AiRaiL". In addition to traffic networking, other facilities will include hotels, offices and a health care centre. In a main concourse area with a glass roof, the entrances to the individual facilities will converge in an interesting shopping arcade.

All of the airport concepts, whether realised or not, represent the wealth of experience and the broad spectrum of skills that the architects from J•S•K use when transforming the wide diversity of requirements and the technical processes of an airport into an attractive, efficiently functioning building. To do this successfully, many disciplines of the airport must be organised, connected and made into a harmonious unit with the architecture. The focal point of all considerations is the people who will use the airport. The economics of the concept and the costs are another important consideration. J•S•K is one of the few companies that are not only capable of planning airports, but also supervising every aspect of a project through to its completion

Every airport poses new challenges. And each time the creativity, innovation and solid know-how of the architects from J•S•K are demanded. Of particular significance is the fact that three major German airports are among the many national and international airport projects J•S•K has carried out with excellent professional competence.

Dr.-Ing. Götz Herberg
Chairman of the Board of
Berlin-Brandenburg Flughafen Holding GmbH
Airport Berlin-Schönefeld

Berlin, in November 2001

Der Mensch steht im Mittelpunkt aller Planungen: Es ist nicht zuletzt dieses Credo, dem die Architekten J•S•K ihre Entwicklung zu einem der bedeutendsten und leistungsstärksten Büros in Deutschland verdanken. Die Entwurfsphilosphie gilt für all ihre Projekte und ganz besonders für die Flughafenplanungen, bei denen die Architekten von J•S•K ihre große Erfahrung und Fachkompetenz unter Beweis stellen.

Die vielfältigen Anforderungen und technischen Abläufe eines Flughafens in ein attraktives Gebäude zu übersetzen, die vielen Disziplinen des Flughafens zu ordnen und mit der Architektur in Einklang zu bringen, ist eine immense Herausforderung. Die Architektur soll dem Menschen, für den der Flughafen Start- und Zielpunkt einer Reise, Arbeitsplatz oder Freizeitvergnügen ist, die Orientierung und Nutzung erleichtern. Bei der Umsetzung dieser Aufgabe bestätigen die Architekten von J•S•K mit jedem neuen Flughafenprojekt ihre Kreativität, Innovation und ihren Sachverstand.

Daß J•S•K einmal national und international zu einem kleinen renommierten Kreis von Architekturbüros gehören würde, die einen Flughafen professionell planen und betreuen können, war 1963 nicht abzusehen. In jenem Jahr gründete der Architekt Helmut Willy Joos das Büro in Frankfurt am Main. Mit der ersten Bauaufgabe am Frankfurter Flughafen, dem Sheraton-Hotel, ging Joos eine Partnerschaft mit Reinhart W. Schulze ein. 1980 gründeten sie gemeinsam mit Karsten Krüger-Heyden das Büro J•S•K Dipl. Ing. Architekten in Frankfurt am Main.

Nach dem Sheraton-Hotel folgten weitere Projekte am und im Frankfurter Flughafen wie das Frankfurt Airport Center oder ein Casino und schließlich das Terminal 2, das eine lichte attraktive Check-In Halle mit einem People Mover erhielt. In den folgenden Jahren kamen weitere Planungen für nationale und internationale Flughafen-Wettbewerbe im In- und Ausland hinzu, und mit ihnen wuchs der ausgezeichnete Ruf der Architekten.

Mit einem attraktiven Konzept gewann J•S•K 1996 den internationalen Wettbewerb am Flughafen Düsseldorf International. Die Architektur des neuen Gebäudes beschreibt den Charakter der Bewegung, die der Flughafen als Knotenpunkt weltweiter Verkehrsströme hervorbringt. Bedeutendster Bestandteil des Konzepts, bei dem bestehende Anlagen in einen Gesamtkomplex eingebunden wurden, ist die Dachkonstruktion. Ihr elliptisches Profil über dem Vorfahrtsbereich des Terminals weckt Assoziationen zum Fliegen. Durch den Einsatz von zeitgenössischen Techniken und Materialien wie Glas und Aluminium entsteht eine Transparenz, welche die eindeutige Architekturhandschrift von J•S•K trägt.

Im Sommer 2001 konnte das neue von einem Journalisten als „Kathedrale des Lichts" bezeichnete Terminal am Flughafen Düsseldorf International in Betrieb gehen. Seitdem erfahren hier Menschen jeden Tag, wie es ist, im Zentrum einer außergewöhnlichen Architektur zu stehen.

Hans-Joachim Peters
Vorsitzender der Geschäftsführung der
Flughafen Düsseldorf GmbH

Düsseldorf, im November 2001

People are the focal point of every design concept. It has not only been this credo that the architects at J•S•K can thank for the fact that they have become one of the most significant and successful firms of architects in Germany, with the highest rate of performance. Our design philosphy applies to all of our projects and especially to the development of airports, which are the ultimate test of the wealth of experience and professional expertise of the architects at J•S•K.

Translating the wide diversity of demands and technical processes of an airport into an attractive building, and organising the many disciplines of the airport and combining these with the architecture are an immense challenge. The architecture should make orientation and utilisation easy for the people using the airport as a starting point and destination of a trip, for those who have their workplace there and for anyone else who spends time there. By achieving these goals, the architects at J•S•K prove their creativitiy, innovation and expertise in every airport project they complete.

Back in 1963 it was hard to imagine that J•S•K would one day belong to an elite circle of national and international firms of architects who are able to professionally plan and carry through airport projects of this dimension. That was the year in which architect Helmut Willy Joos founded the company in Frankfurt / Main. With their first construction job at Frankfurt Airport, the Sheraton Hotel, Joos entered in a partnership with Reinhart W. Schulze. In 1980, together with Karsten Krüger-Heyden, they founded J•S•K Dipl. Ing. Architekten in Frankfurt/Main.

The Sheraton Hotel was followed by other projects in and around Frankfurt Airport, including the Frankfurt Airport Centre, a casino and then Terminal 2, which was given a light and attractive check-in hall with a People Mover. The following years brought further design concepts for national and international airport competitions in Germany and abroad, and with each winning concept the excellent reputation of the architects was further enhanced.

In 1996 J•S•K won the international competition for the rebuilding of Düsseldorf International Airport with an attractive design concept. The architecture of the new building reflects the character of movement of the airport as a hub of global transportation. The most important component of the concept is its roof construction, which connects the buildings to make a unified complex. Its elliptical profile over the entrance of the terminal triggers associations with flying. The use of contemporary technologies and materials, such as glass and aluminium, creates a transparency which bears the distinctive architectural style of J•S•K.

In the summer of 2001 the new terminal, described by a journalist as a "cathedral of light", was opened for business at Düsseldorf International Airport. Since then, people experience here every day what it is like to stand in the midst of extraordinary architecture.

Hans-Joachim Peters
Chairman of the Board of
Flughafen Düsseldorf GmbH

Düsseldorf, in November 2001

Einleitung
Karsten Krüger Heyden

In der im Jahr 2000 publizierten Werkschau unseres Büros, „J•S•K Architekten. Gebaute Transparenz", die in einem vergleichenden Überblick das gesamte Spektrum der Bauaufgaben umfaßte, mit denen wir uns beschäftigen, stand die Herausarbeitung der Gemeinsamkeiten im Vordergrund, die unsere Architektur unabhängig von unterschiedlichen Aufgabenstellungen bestimmen. Nachdem wir mit dieser Zusammenschau unser Grundkonzept und unsere Zielsetzungen verdeutlicht haben, erschien es sinnvoll, einzelne Schwerpunkte unseres Schaffens umfassender und vertiefter darzustellen.

Flughäfen – als Knotenpunkte weltweiter Verkehrsströme – zählen auch von ihrer Dimension her zu unseren anspruchsvollsten und zugleich zukunftsträchtigsten Projekten, weshalb es naheliegt, gerade ihnen einen eigenen Band zu widmen. Die besondere Herausforderung bei ihnen besteht darin, ein Höchstmaß an Funktionalität und Wirtschaftlichkeit adäquat in ein modernes ästhetisch ausgereiftes Gesamtkonzept einzubauen und die entstehenden Großbauten wiederum der vorhandenen Umgebung anzupassen. Angesichts der Bedeutung solcher Verkehrsknotenpunkte für die heutige mobile Gesellschaft sind sie außerdem auch als repräsentative Bauten mit jeweils eigener Identität zu verstehen und zu gestalten.

An dieser Stelle sei mir erlaubt, kurz zu skizzieren, welche Grundbedingungen einen Großflughafen im wesentlichen bestimmen. Jeder große Airport hat hochtechnisierte Anforderungen zu erfüllen, man denke z. B. an die Gepäckabfertigung: Das Gepäckstück wird auf Transportbändern über mehrere Geschosse vom Check-In-Schalter zur Gepäcksortiermaschine (Sorter) transportiert. Bei Abflugsverzögerungen oder Weiterflügen muß es auf Warteschleifen der Bänder aufbewahrt werden. Vom Flugzeug, das auf Position steht, wird das Gepäck ebenfalls in einen Sorter gebracht und entweder zur Gepäckausgabe oder zu einem Anschlußflug weitergeleitet. Jedes Gepäckstück wird nach der Aufgabe am Check-In-Schalter von einem zentralen Sicherheitsgerät geprüft.

Der Passagier – ob er ankommt oder abfliegt – ist mit den dazugehörigen Funktionsabläufen der wichtigste Bezugspunkt für die Planung von Großflughäfen. Seine Orientierung kann durch Blickkontakt zum jeweiligen Außenraum verbessert werden. Die Wege, die er zurücklegt, sollten klar gegliedert, Ebenenwechsel vermieden werden. Wenn dies nicht möglich ist, ist darauf zu achten, daß sie vertikal nur in eine Richtung gehen. Eine sinnvolle, quasi natürliche Wegführung im Flughafen erleichtert das Reisen und erhöht die Akzeptanz des Flughafens.

Eine weitere Komponente in der Planung ist heute die ausgedehnte Konsumsektion in allen Funktionsbereichen des Airports. Im Abflugs- und Ankunftsbereich muß sie neben den Passagieren auch von normalen Kunden genutzt werden können. Darüber hinaus sind weitere Laden- und Restaurationsflächen auf der Abflugebene nach der Sicherheits- bzw. nach der Paßkontrolle vorzusehen, die nur dem Passagier zugänglich

sind. Hotels, Konferenz- und Einkaufszentren wie auch Bürogebäude ergänzen die Dienstleistungs- und Konsumzonen.

Ein Großflughafen wird heute nicht nur über eine Autobahn oder Autobahnzubringer erschlossen, sondern benötigt auch einen Flughafenbahnhof, in dem nicht nur die Flughafenzubringerzüge aus der Stadt halten, sondern auch die schnellen nationalen und internationalen Expreßzüge, so daß Schiene, Auto und Flugzeug miteinander verknüpft sind.

Wenn ein Flughafen über die Größe, die ein Passagier zu Fuß oder mit Hilfe von Walkways in angemessener Zeit bewältigen kann, hinauswächst oder aus mehreren Terminals besteht, werden vollautomatische Kabinenbahnen, sog. People Mover, zur schnellen Beförderung der Passagiere eingesetzt. Sie dienen auch dazu, Flughafenterminals und Flughafenbahnhof zu verbinden. Die Trassenführung für den People Mover kann oberirdisch wie unterirdisch erfolgen und benötigt entsprechende vertikale Anbindungen bis zur People-Mover-Station.

Aus der Vielzahl der komplexen Anforderungen an einen Flughafen können hier nur einige wichtige Punkte herausgegriffen werden. Der Leser und Betrachter wird sie auf den folgenden Seiten in den von J•S•K entwickelten Flughäfen wiederfinden. Eine detailliertere Beschreibung und Erörterung der Thematik würde den Umfang eines solchen Buchs sprengen.

In diesem Band werden realisierte und laufende Projekte präsentiert wie der Ausbau bzw. die Neukonzeptionierung deutscher und europäischer Flughäfen – so in Frankfurt, Düsseldorf, Berlin oder auch Athen – sowie Wettbewerbsbeiträge für deutsche, europäische und auch asiatische Flughafenprojekte – so in Hongkong und Shanghai. Damit soll verdeutlicht werden, wie die Grundsätze unseres Arbeitens bei dieser spezifischen Bauaufgabe umgesetzt werden. Auch hier sehen wir es als unsere Sache an, ein Projekt möglichst in all seinen Phasen – von den ersten Vorskizzen bis zur Fertigstellung und den kleinsten Details – mitzuentwickeln, was eine enge und konstruktive Zusammenarbeit mit allen am Planungsprozeß Beteiligten, vor allem mit den Auftraggebern bedingt.

Unsere Entwürfe und Planungen vermeiden auch bei den komplizierten technischen und funktionalen Zusammenhängen eines Flughafens jede unnötige Komplexität und bemühen sich um eine homogene einfache und präzise Architektursprache, gekennzeichnet von Transparenz in jedem Sinne des Wortes. Denn im Mittelpunkt der architektonischen Planung steht für uns stets in erster Linie der Mensch, insbesondere der Flugreisende, dem klare Bezugspunkte und eine durchdachte Verkehrsführung den Weg weisen sollen.

Für das Vertrauen, das uns alle an den Flughafenplanungen Beteiligte entgegengebracht haben, sowie die gute Zusammenarbeit möchten wir uns an dieser Stelle herzlich bedanken. Unser Dank gilt auch dem Verlag, den Autoren sowie den Mitarbeitern bei der Zusammenstellung des Buchs, insbesondere auch meinem Partner Herrn Helmut W. Joos.

Karsten Krüger Heyden

In the first publication about our firm, which came out in the year 2000 entitled "J•S•K Architekten. Built Transparency", and which encompasses the entire spectrum of our architectural projects in a comparative overview the focus was mainly on the common denominators that define our architecture regardless of the varying types of challenges we are facing. Having clearly outlined our basic concepts and our main objectives in this synopsis, it seemed a good idea to represent individual focal points of our achievements more comprehensively and in greater detail in a second book.

Airports – as transport hubs for global traffic – are among our most demanding and at the same time future-oriented projects, not least due to their superlative dimensions. Therefore it makes sense to dedicate a special book to them alone. The special challenges associated with airport projects require the highest degree of functionality and economics, imbedded in modern aesthetics and a perfectly developed overall concept for buildings that fit in well in their surroundings. In view of the significance of such transport hubs for today's mobile society, they must also be regarded and designed as representative structures each with its own identity.

At this point I would like to briefly outline the basic conditions that determine major airports. Every big airport must fulfil high technological specifications – just think, for example, of the baggage handling. Each piece of luggage is carried on conveyor belts over numerous levels from the check-in counter to the baggage sorter. If take-off is delayed or in the case of connecting flights, it must be kept in a waiting stack on the conveyor belt. From the aircraft in its docking position outside the airport the baggage must also be brought in to the sorter and either passed on to the baggage claim area or to the connecting flight. Every piece of luggage that is checked in must first be examined by a central security scanning device.

The passenger and all functions pertaining to the passenger – whether arriving or departing – are the most important point of reference for the planning of major airports. Passenger orientation can be improved by providing the possibility of eye contact to the exterior. The walkways that lead him to his destination should be clearly demarcated, and the necessity of changing floors should be avoided. As this is often not possible, his route must planned so that, vertically speaking, he must only go in one direction. Logical and quasi natural directional signs in the airport make travelling easier for the passenger and enhance his acceptance of the airport.

A further component in airport development today is the extensive consumerism in all functional areas of the airport. In the departures and arrivals areas these facilities must be accessible not only to passengers but to regular consumers as well. Additional shops and restaurants must be provided on the departures level after the security and passport check points, which are only accessible to passengers with boarding

tickets. Hotels, conference and shopping centres, as well office buildings complete the services and consumer areas.

The major airport of today is not only connected to a motorway or access ramp. It also needs an airport railway station which is not only serviced by airport express trains from the city, but also by high speed national and international express trains, so that rail, road and air transportation systems are efficiently linked.

If an airport becomes so big that a passenger can no longer cover the necessary distance via walkways in a reasonable amount of time or if it has several terminals, fully automated vehicles on overhead rails, so-called People Movers, are used to transfer the passengers quickly and conveniently. They also serve as a connecting link between the airport terminals and the airport railway station. The rail system for the People Mover can either be built above or below ground and requires a vertical connection to the People Mover station.

But of the large number of complex demands made on an airport, only a few important points can be touched on here. You, the reader, will find these on the following pages in the airports development projects of J•S•K. A more detailed description and examination of this topic would hardly fit into a book of this size.

This volume presents both realised and current projects, such as the expansion and restructuring of German and European airports – in Frankfurt, Düsseldorf, Berlin and even Athens – as well as competition design concepts for German, European and even Asian airport projects – in Hong Kong and Shanghai. This is intended to emphasise how the basic principles of our work are implemented into such specific development projects. And here again, we consider it our business to develop every project, if possible, in all its phases – from the first draft sketches to the last finishing touch, right down to the smallest detail. This requires close and constructive collaboration with everyone involved in the planning process, in particular the customer.

Our drafts and concepts avoid any unnecessary complexity, even in the face of the complicated technical and functional relationships of an airport, and we try to achieve a homogeneously simple and precise architectural language, characterised by transparency in every sense of the word. Because for us, people are the most important consideration of architectural planning – in particular airline passengers, for whom clear points of reference and a well-planned directional system must be provided.

For the trust we have received from everyone involved in our airport development projects, and for the positive collaboration with them, we express our heartfelt thanks. Our thanks also go to the publisher, the authors and all the others who contributed to the making of this book, in particular my partner Helmut W. Joos.

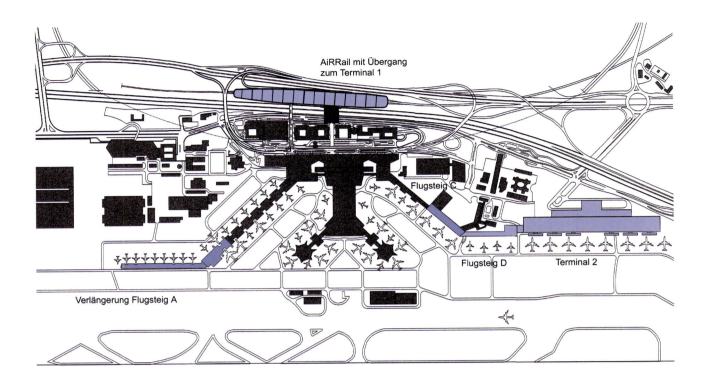

Der Frankfurter Flughafen ist nicht nur eine Drehscheibe des Luftverkehrs im Zentrum Europas, sondern einer der wichtigsten Knotenpunkte weltweiter Verkehrsströme, nicht nur für Passagiere, sondern auch für Frachtgüter. Diese müssen über ein leistungsfähiges Zubringer- und Verteilersystem mit dem Interkontinentalverkehr vernetzt werden. Um den wachsenden Anforderungen gerecht zu werden, wurde der Flughafen im Laufe des 20. Jahrhunderts immer wieder erweitert.

Zwischen 1989 und 1995 wurde das Terminal 1 von J•S•K durch den Neubau des Terminals 2 ergänzt. Das neue Terminal ist über eine Erweiterung des alten Flugsteigs C und den neuen Flugsteig D, der als Bindeglied zwischen der Verlängerung und dem Neubau fungiert, an das alte Dreifinger-Terminal 1 angeschlossen. Darüber hinaus gibt es zwischen Terminal 2 und der alten Passagierabfertigungsanlage ein vollautomatisches Passagier-Transfer-System (PTS).

Das neue Terminal richtet sich nach der linearen Anordnung der Flugzeugstandorte. Das sog. lineare Terminal nutzt die zur Verfügung stehende Grundstücksfläche optimal aus. Durch den neuen Fernbahnhof AiRail ist der Frankfurter Flughafen jetzt direkt an das europäische Hochgeschwindigkeitsnetz der Bahn angeschlossen. Die Verbindung zwischen Luftfahrt, Schiene und Individualverkehr ist mit dem neuen Fernbahnhof geschaffen.

Frankfurt Airport is not only Germany's most important gateway for continental and intercontinental air transportation, but also Europe's most important international transport hub – not only for passengers, but also for air freight. As an intermodal transportation centre, Frankfurt Airport links intercontinental traffic via a high-performance transportation system. Over the course of the 20th century the airport was repeatedly expanded to meet growing demands.

Between 1989 and 1995, Terminal 1 was supplemented by J•S•K through the addition of Terminal 2. The new terminal is connected to the old three-pier Terminal 1 through an extension of the old Pier C and the addition of the new Pier D, which functions as a link between the extension and the new terminal building. Additionally, a fully automated Passenger Transfer System (PTS) now operates between Terminal 2 and the old passenger check-in area.

The new terminal is streamlined to the linear arrangement of the aircraft docking positions. The so-called linear terminal makes optimum use of all available ground space. Thanks to the new AirRail railway station, Frankfurt Airport now has the best rail connections of any airport in Europe, with a direct link to the high-speed train network. The new railway station completes the link between air, rail and road transportation.

Check-in-Halle Terminal 2
Blick vom Vorfeld auf den Terminal 2

Check-in hall, Terminal 2
View of Terminal 2 from the apron

Die ersten Planungen, die Ende 1988 begonnen wurden, sahen zunächst ein Terminal für Auslandsflüge mit mehreren Parkebenen auf dem Dach vor. Nach einer Umplanung wurden die Parkplätze in eine Tiefgarage vor das Terminal verlegt. 1994 während der Bauzeit wurde das Schengener Abkommen eingeführt, das weitere Umplanungen bzw. Umbauten nach sich zog. Getrennte Ebenen für Schengen- und Non-Schengen-Passagiere mit den dazugehörigen Warteräumen wurden im Terminal notwendig. Bisher hatte die Planung eine Ankunftsebene und eine Abflugsebene für internationale Flüge vorgesehen.

Das fertiggestellte Terminal mit landseitiger Einebenenvorfahrt und acht Gebäude- sowie weiteren 18 Vorfeldpositionen verfügt über eine Kapazität von 14 Millionen Passagieren im Jahr. Der Neubau ist ein etwa 600 Meter langer, 120 Meter breiter und ab Vorfeld über 30 Meter hoher symmetrischer Baukörper. Gegliedert wird dieser in eine Check-In-Halle und die mehrgeschossigen Passagierankunfts- und -abflugsbereiche, die sich zum Vorfeld hin orientieren. Im Zentrum der symmetrischen Anlage über der Vorfahrt liegt der PTS-Bahnhof, der sich aus dem überdachten Baukörper herausschiebt.

Rechts und links des Terminals sind zwei Bürohäuser angefügt, die vom Vorfeld aus gesehen hinter den Ankunfts- und Abflugsbereichen der Schengen-Passagiere liegen. Besonderes Charakteristikum des Gebäudes ist – außen wie innen – sein markantes Dach, das alle Funktionen und Nutzungen überdacht und verbindet. Die spektakuläre Dachkonstruktion erinnert in ihrer architektonischen Ausbildung an die Bahnhöfe zu Beginn des vorigen Jahrhunderts.

Das vormontierte weitgespannte Flächentragwerk liegt auf mächtigen Kernen auf, welche die Erschließung der verschiedenen Geschoßebenen und die Technikschächte aufnehmen. Die Treppenhäuser in den Kernen dienen auch als Fluchtwege, die in einen unterirdischen Fluchttunnel münden. Das Tragwerk des zentralen Dachs über den Passagierabfertigungsbereichen ist als segmentförmige Rundbögen gestaltet, die es architektonisch betonen. Die übrigen Gebäudeteile ordnen sich dem großen Dach unter und haben flache Dächer. Die filigrane Konstruktion genügt allen technisch-funktionalen Anforderungen und ist gleichzeitig auch ein gestalterisches Moment.

Die Oberlichter des Dachs sorgen zusammen mit den transparenten Fassaden für einen hohen Tageslichtanteil im Terminal. Diese großflächige Verglasung erleichtert dem Passagier die Orientierung in den Abfertigungsbereichen. Er bewegt sich in klar gegliederten, lichtdurchfluteten Raumbereichen, was zu seinem Wohlbefinden beiträgt. Die Fassaden haben Sonnenschutzverglasung und sind teilweise zum Vorfeld mit Radardämpfungsmaßnahmen ausgestattet. Durch ihre Klarheit trägt auch die von ihren Dimensionen her eindrucksvolle, 28 Meter hohe Check-In-Halle zur hervorragenden Orientierung im Gebäude bei.

Auf der Ebene 2, auf der auch die Einebenenvorfahrt liegt, befindet sich die Check-In-Halle und der Ankunfts- und Abflugsbereich für die Schengen-Passagiere. Die Warteräume für die Schengen-Passagiere wurden während der Bauzeit neu konzipiert, sie sind als Pavillons angebunden und zwischen die Flugsteige der Gebäudepositionen vor die Fassade des Terminalgebäudes gestellt. Zwei Gepäckausgaben mit jeweils sechs Gepäckbändern und die Zollabfertigung sind symmetrisch zur Mittelachse und zur Ankunftshalle auf der Ebene 2 in Richtung Vorfeld angeordnet.

Der Abflugsbereich der Non-Schengen-Passagiere mit den dazugehörigen Sicherheits- und Paßkontrollen und den Warteräumen liegt auf der Ebene 3, an die auch die Gebäudepositionen über Fluggaststege angebunden sind. Die Ankunft der Non-Schengen-Passagiere erfolgt ebenfalls auf der Ebene 3, und die Passagiere werden dann über Rolltreppen in die Ebene 2 zu den Gepäckausgabebereichen geführt. Auf den Ebenen 2 und 3 befinden sich Verkaufsflächen für die abfliegenden Passagiere.

Auf der Ebene 1 unter den Hauptgeschossen liegt die Gepäckabfertigung mit dem zentralen Sorter. Über diesem Bereich enthält eine abgetrennte Ebene die Gepäcktransportbänder. Die Gepäcksortiermaschine im Erdgeschoß kann für 24 Stunden ein Notlaufprogramm für die Gepäckabfertigung des gesamten Flughafens Frankfurt übernehmen.

Auf der Ebene 4 über den Passagierwarteräumen der Non-Schengen-Passagiere finden sich gastronomische Einrichtungen und die Besucherterrasse mit Blick auf das Vorfeld. Der PTS-Bahnhof ist auf den Ebenen 3 und 4 über der Vorfahrt angesiedelt. Die Fahrzeuge des Passagier-Transfer-Systems, dessen Trasse ebenfalls über den Vorfahrten liegt, werden vollautomatisch gesteuert. Sie verbinden die beiden Terminals des Frankfurter Flughafens miteinander und gewährleisten Umsteigezeiten von maximal 45 Minuten.

Der Charakter der zentralen Abfertigungshalle wird durch eine geringe Anzahl von Materialien und Farben bestimmt. Zurückhaltend und elegant wirken der polierte Granit des Bodens und die hellen geflammten Granitplatten, mit denen die Gebäudekerne verkleidet sind. Die Farbwahl der Materialien wurde bewußt zurückhaltend gewählt, da durch die Passagiere und die vielfältigen Wegweiser und Reklameträger noch unterschiedliche Farbtöne in das Gesamtensemble der Halle eingebracht werden.

The initial development project, begun at the end of 1988, included a new terminal for international flights with several parking levels on the roof. However, the concept was revised and the parking facilities were moved to an underground car park in front of the terminal. While construction was in progress in 1994, the Schengen Agreement was introduced, which resulted in further changes and/or rebuilding measures. According to the agreement separate levels for Schengen and non-Schengen passengers, each with their own waiting areas, were required in the terminal. Until then the plans for the terminal had included an arrivals level and a departures level for all intercontinental and international flights.

The completed terminal with a single-level road access system, eight gate areas and a further 18 docking positions on the apron, can handle a capacity of 14 million passengers a year. The new building is a symmetrical construction, around 600 metres in length, 120 metres wide and over 30 metres high on the terminal apron side. The building is divided into a check-in hall and multilevel passenger arrival and departure areas, all of which face the airfield. Situated in the centre of the symmetrical construction above the access road is the People Transfer System (PTS) terminal, which extends over the roof structure.

To the right and left of the terminal are two office blocks, which, when viewed from the terminal apron, are situated behind the arrivals and departures areas for Schengen passengers. A particular characteristic of the building – from both the outside and the inside – is its distinctive roof, which tops and joins all of the functions and facilities of the building. The architectonic formation of the spectacular roof construction is reminiscent of railway stations at the beginning of the last century.

The pre-assembled wide-spanned load-bearing structure is supported by mighty core elements, which contain the cable ducts and other technology for the various floors. The staircases in the core elements also serve as emergency escape exits, which converge in an underground emergency escape tunnel. The supportive girders of the central roof over the concourse form a segmented round arch, which underscores the architectonic design of the structure. This main roof extends over the other sections of the building, each with its own flat roof. The intricate construction not only meets all technical and functional requirements, but also provides an artistic element.

The skylights in the ceiling, together with the transparent façades of the building, provide generous amounts of daylight in the terminal. The transparency of the glass also makes it easier for passengers to orient themselves in the check-in areas. In such clearly demarcated, light and airy spaces, every passenger feels an increased sense of well-being. The tinted glass of the façades filter the sunlight and some of the façades on the apron side are also equipped with radar reflectors. Added

clarity for excellent orientation in the building is provided by the impressive dimensions of the 28 metre-high ceilings of the concourse where the check-in counters are situated.

On Level 2, where the single-level access road system is also located, is the check-in hall with the arrivals and departures areas for Schengen passengers. The reconstruction measures also included the redesigning of the waiting lounges for Schengen passengers, which are now in pavilions situated between the gate areas outside the terminal building. Two baggage claim halls, each with six baggage carousels and customs check points, are arranged symmetrically to the central axis and to the arrivals area on Level 2, on the terminal apron side.

The departures area for non-Schengen passengers, with separate security and passport control and waiting areas, is situated on Level 3, which is connected to the gate areas via passenger walkways. The arrival area for non-Schengen passengers is also situated on Level 3 and from there the passengers reach the baggage claim hall on Level 2 by escalator. On Levels 2 and 3 are shopping areas for departing passengers.

On Level 1 below the main floors is the baggage processing area with the central baggage sorter. A separate level above this contains the baggage carousels. The baggage sorting machine on the ground floor can take over the baggage processing operations for the entire Frankfurt Airport for 24 hours in case of emergency.

On Level 4, above the waiting areas for non-Schengen passengers, are restaurants and snack bars and the spectators' terrace with a view of the airfield. The PTS terminal is located on Levels 3 and 4 above the access road. The vehicles of the Passenger Transfer System, whose route also follows the airport access roads, are fully automated. They connect both terminals of the Frankfurt Airport to one another and guarantee transfer times of no more than 45 minutes.

The character of the main check-in hall is determined by the reduction of materials and colour in its design. A reserved and elegant atmosphere is created by the polished granite of the floor and the light-coloured variegated granite tiles lining the inside walls of the building. The carefully selected colours of the materials used are purposefully kept to a minimum, as the passengers and the many information signs and ads on the walls add a wide variety of colour shades to the overall colour scheme of the concourse area.

Entwurfsvariante: Parken auf dem Dach
Ansicht Vorfahrt
Ansichten der Baustelle

Concept variation: parking on the roof
View of access road
View of the construction site

Flughafen Frankfurt am Main, Terminal 2

Flughafen Frankfurt am Main, Terminal 2

Vorfahrt mit PTS
Check-In-Halle
Abflug

Check-In mit Gepäckaufgabe
Check-In-Halle

Access road with PTS
Check-in hall
Departures

Check-in counters with baggage check-in
Check-in hall

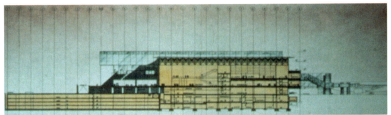

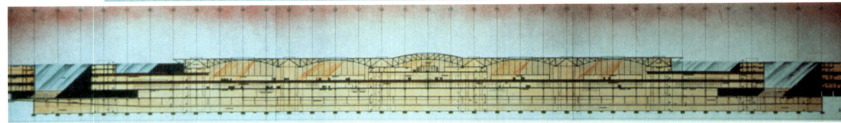

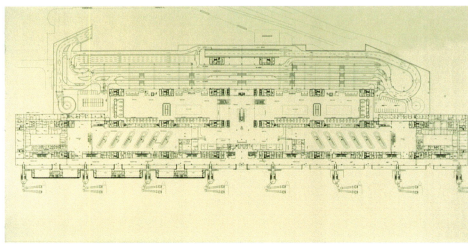

Flughafen Frankfurt am Main, Terminal 2

Quer- und Längsschnitt mit PTS
Warteraum Ankunft
Grundriß Schengen-Warteraum

Gepäckband
Gepäckausgabe

Cross- and longitudinal section with PTS
Waiting room in Arrivals
Floor plan of Schengen waiting room

Baggage carousel
Baggage claim hall

28

Food Plaza
Aufgang Food Plaza,

Sicherheitskontrolle
Wartebereich
Wartebereich

Food plaza
Escalators to food plaza,

Security check point
Waiting area
Waiting area

Flughafen Frankfurt am Main, Terminal 2

Flughafen Frankfurt am Main, Terminal 2

Läden Ankunft International
Verbindungsgang

Blick Innenhof Bürogebäude
Verbindungsgang

Shops international arrivals
Connecting walkway

View of office building lobby
Connecting walkway

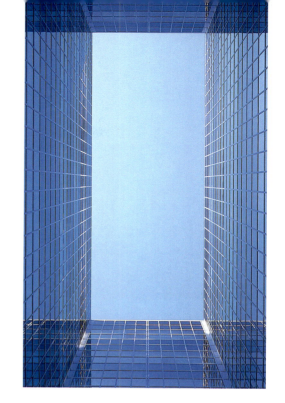

Fassade Vorfahrt
PTS-Bahnhof
PTS bei Einfahrt

Innenaufnahme mit
Blick auf vorbeifahrenden PTS

Façade on access road side
PTS station
PTS vehicle approaching terminal

Photo inside terminal with
view of passing PTS vehicle

Flughafen Frankfurt am Main, Terminal 2

Fassadenecklösung
Blick von der Besucherterrasse
   auf das Vorfeld
Terminal 2 vom Vorfeld
Seitlicher Bürotrakt

Passagierstege
Terminal Ost

Façade corner design
View from the spectators' terrace
   over the apron
Terminal 2 from the apron
Side view of office block

Passenger walkways
East terminal

Flughafen Frankfurt am Main, Terminal 2

Flughafen Frankfurt am Main, Terminal 2

Verbindungsgang zu den Gates A–C
Connecting walkway to Gates A–C

Der C-Finger von Terminal 1 wurde zwischen 1996 und 1998 erweitert und verlängert. Der ca. 475 Meter lange, 75 Meter breite und 20 Meter hohe Bau verfügt nach der Umgestaltung über neun Gates und vier weitere Positionen auf dem Vorfeld, auf der Ebene 2 über Lounges, Sozialräume und Airlinebüros sowie auf der Abflugebene 3 über Sammelwarteräume für Schengen- und Non-Schengen-Passagiere.

Die Einrichtungen für den Gate-Check-In und die Busgateabgänge befinden sich auf gleichem Niveau wie im Terminal 1. Der Flugsteig C wird durch die Check-In-Flächen und Gepäckausgabebänder im Terminal 1 versorgt. Darunter verteilen sich auf den Ebenen 0 und 1 Versorgungseinrichtungen, Service-, Lager- und Technikflächen bzw. Werkstätten. Da das Gebäude auch über Gatepositionen und eine Verbindung zu Warteräumen für High-Risk-Passagiere verfügt, ist seine Fassade weitgehend geschlossen.

Der verlängerte Flugsteig, in dem noch Einrichtungen für die Paß- und Zollkontrolle geschaffen wurden, bildet nun – mit dem anschließenden Flugsteig D – eine direkte Verbindung zwischen Terminal 1 und Terminal 2, vermittelt aber nicht nur funktional, sondern auch durch seine architektonische Gestalt zwischen diesen beiden.

Between 1996 and 1998, Pier C of Terminal 1 was widened and extended in length. Since its reconstruction, the approx. 475-metre long, 75-metre wide and 20-metre high building has nine gates and four further aircraft positions on the terminal apron, lounges, public facilities and airline offices on Level 2 as well as central waiting rooms for Schengen and non-Schengen passengers on Departures Level 3.

The equipment for the gate check-in counters and the bus gate exits are located on the same level as in Terminal 1. Pier C uses the check-in and the baggage claim halls in Terminal 1. Below this, on Levels 0 and 1 are the utilities, service and storage areas as well as rooms for technical equipment and workshops for the technicians. As the building also has it own gate areas and a direct link to the waiting lounges for high-risk passengers, its façades are largely closed.

The extended pier, which contains the equipment for passport and customs screening, now forms a direct link between Terminal 1 and Terminal 2 together with the adjacent Pier D, and forms a connection between the two, not only in terms of function but also through its architectonic design.

Längsblick D-Finger

Überblick C-Finger, D-Finger und
Terminal 2

Lengthwise view of Pier D

*Aerial view of Pier C, Pier D and
Terminal 2*

Mit Flugsteig D, der zwischen 1996 und 1997 errichtet wurde
und sich formal wie funktionsmäßig westlich an das neuent-
standene Terminal 2 des Frankfurter Flughafens anschließt,
dieses gewissermaßen fortsetzt, wurde die letzte Lücke in der
Linie, die von Terminal 1 über den gleichzeitig verlängerten
Flugsteig C zum neuen Terminal 2 führt, geschlossen. Auf
diesem Weg können die Passagiere nun auch zu Fuß von einem Terminal zum anderen gelangen.
Der etwa 320 Meter lange, 20 Meter hohe und im wesentlichen
21 Meter breite neue Flugsteig kann jährlich bis zu 5 Millionen
Passagiere abfertigen. Er bedient fünf Gate- und acht Vorfeld-
positionen. Die Gebäudegates werden vom Terminal 2 aus er-
schlossen, und der Check-In- und der Gepäckausgabebereich
vom Terminal 2 bedienen die Flugzeugpositionen im D-Finger.
Flugsteig D verfügt über getrennte Ebenen für Schengen- und
Non-Schengen-Passagiere mit Warteräumen und Lounges.
Über dem Abfertigungsbereich der Passagiere befindet sich ein
Bürotrakt.
In seiner Fassade greift der Flugsteig Elemente von Terminal 2
wieder auf und bildet gestalterisch dessen Fortsetzung.

*Pier D was built between 1996 and 1997, and is situated on
the west side of the newly-built Terminal 2 of Frankfurt Airport. This new pier continues the design and function of the
new terminal building and fills the last gap in the line that
runs between Terminal 1 and the new Terminal 2 via Pier C,
which was also extended at the same time. Passengers can
now walk conveniently from one terminal to the other.
The new pier, approx. 320 metres long, 20 metres high and
essentially 21 metres across, can accommodate up to 5 million passengers a year. It serves five gates and eight apron
positions. The gate areas of Pier D with a direct connection to
Terminal 2, are serviced by the check-in counters and baggage claim hall in Terminal 2. Pier D has separate levels for
Schengen and non-Schengen passengers, each with waiting
areas and lounges. Above the check-in area for passengers is
an office block.
The façade of Pier D reflects the architectural elements of
Terminal 2 and forms a continuation of its artistic design.*

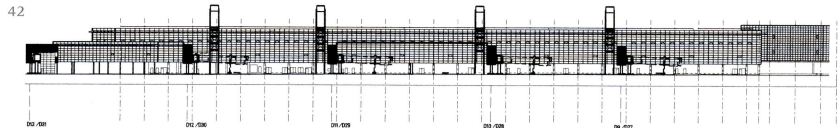

Ansicht
D-Finger und Terminal 2
Lounge

C- und D-Finger Verbindungsgang
Check-In-Schalter
Ansicht vom Vorfeld

Front view
Pier D and Terminal 2
Lounge

Pier C and D connecting walkway
Check-in counters
View from the apron

Flughafen Frankfurt am Main, Flugsteig D

Flughafen Frankfurt am Main, Verlängerung Flugsteig A

Um für die Abfertigung der Lufthansa zusätzliche Kapazitäten zu schaffen, wurde der A-Finger des Terminals 1 des Frankfurter Flughafens zwischen Dezember 1997 und Februar 2000 um ca. 500 Meter verlängert. Mit dem Erweiterungsbau wurden 12 neue Gebäudepositionen mit Gate-Check-In-Schaltern, Warteräumen und Geschäften geschaffen. Die Kapazität der Verlängerung des A-Fingers beträgt 6 Millionen Passagiere. Das langgestreckte riegelartige Gebäude, das in eine Schengen- und Non-Schengen-Ebene mit den entsprechenden Warteräumen aufgeteilt ist, verfügt über eine Bruttogeschoßfläche von ca. 55.000 m² und einen Bruttorauminhalt von ca. 265.000 m³, die sich im wesentlichen auf die drei Hauptgeschosse verteilen.

Während die Haustechnik und der Bodenservice für das Gepäck auf der Vorfeldebene 01 liegen, befinden sich die Passagierbereiche auf den Ebenen 02 und 03, Ebene 02 hat neben den entsprechenden Gatewartezonen auch Lounges, Ebene 03 erhielt darüber hinaus Büroräume und die Einsatzzentrale der Lufthansa.

Auf dem Flugsteig A wurde die räumliche Hülle eines PTS-Bahnhofs vorgerüstet. Bisher ist dieser aber noch nicht an das PTS-System angeschlossen.

Between December 1997 and February 2000, Pier A of Terminal 1 of Frankfurt Airport was extended by about 500 metres in order to create additional capacity for loading and servicing Lufthansa flights. This extension created 12 additional docking positions, each with gate check-in counters, waiting areas and shops. The extension of Pier A has created a total handling capacity of 6 million passengers per year. This elongated, narrow building, which is divided into Schengen and non-Schengen levels each with its own waiting lounges, encompasses a gross floor space per level of approx. 55,000 m² with a gross capacity of approx. 265,000 m³ distributed over the three main levels.

While building services and ground services for baggage processing are situated on the apron Level 01, the passenger handling areas are on Levels 02 and 03. In addition to the usual gate waiting areas, Level 02 also has lounges, and Level 03 now contains additional office space and the Lufthansa operational centre.

The basic framework for a People Transfer System terminal was erected on the roof of Pier A. To date this PTS terminal has not yet been connected to the existing PTS system.

Aufgang PTS-Bahnhof
Verbindungsgang
Wartebereich Lufthansa
Blick vom Vorfeld

Wartebereich Lufthansa
Verlängerung A-Finger

Entrance to PTS station
Connecting walkway
Lufthansa waiting area
View from the apron

Lufthansa waiting area
Extension of Pier A

Was das Luftfrachtaufkommen angeht, so steht der Frankfurter Flughafen heute in Europa an erster Stelle. Um diese Position zu wahren, wurde in den 90er Jahren, als die bestehenden Flächenkapazitäten knapp zu werden begannen und nachdem die amerikanische Airbase diesen Bereich freigemacht hatte, südlich des bereits vorhandenen Flughafenbereichs eine neue Frachtabfertigung mit dem Namen CargoCity Süd konzipiert.

J•S•K baute hier von 1996 bis 1997 auf einem Gesamtareal von 320.000 m² zwei 48.000 m² große Frachthallen, außerdem zwei Bürogebäude mit je 10.000 m², das Fracht- und Logistikzentrum, einen Werkstattbau mit Batterieladestation sowie ein Parkhaus mit Kantine.

Die Architektur der Hallen wird außen von den in regelmäßigen Abständen sichtbaren Pylonmasten, an denen die Dächer aufgehängt sind, geprägt. Die beiden langgestreckten, flachgedeckten, siebengeschossigen Bürogebäude haben horizontal gegliederte, hinterlüftete Aluminium-Glas-Fassaden. Das Erdgeschoß ist an einer der beiden Gebäudeseiten hinter einer Arkade leicht zurückversetzt. Im Innern wurde auf größtmögliche Flexibilität in der Grundrißgestaltung der elektronisch hochwertig ausgestatteten Büroräume geachtet. Die großzügigen Fensterflächen bieten eine gute Sicht über das Flugfeld.

In terms of air cargo volume, Frankfurt Airport is Europe's largest freight airport today. In order to maintain this position, in the 1990s, when the existing space capacity began to run short and after the American airbase had moved out of the area, a new cargo processing centre, called "CargoCity Süd" was built south of the already existing airport area. From 1996 to 1997, J•S•K built two 48,000 m² cargo halls here on a total area of 320,000 m², as well as two office buildings, each with 10,000 m² of area space, a cargo and logistics centre, a workshop building with a battery recharging station and a car park with a cafeteria.

The architecture of the halls is characterised from the outside by highly visible pylon masts, which support the roofs at regular intervals. Both of the elongated, flat-roofed, seven-storey office buildings have horizontally-sectioned, rear-ventilated aluminium and glass façades. On one side of the building the ground floor is set back slightly behind an arcade. Inside the buildings, the highest possible level of flexibility has been integrated into the floor plan of the offices, which are equipped with state-of-the-art electronic equipment. The large windows offer an excellent view of the airfield.

Halle B1
Bürogebäude BB1

Fracht- und Logistikzentrum, Schrägansicht
Fracht- und Logistikzentrum, Südseite
Bürogebäude mit Stichpier der Halle B1
Stichpier der Halle B2

Hall B1
Office building BB1

Freight and logistics centre, oblique view
Freight and logistics centre, south side
Office building with branch pier of Hall B1
Branch pier of Hall B2

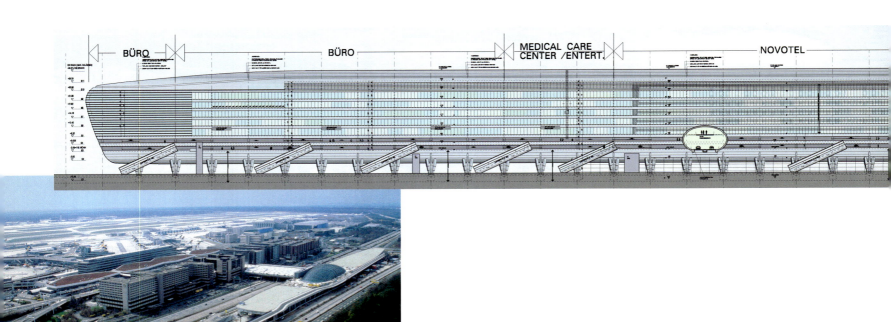

1999 gewann J•S•K in einem kombinierten Investoren- und Architektenwettbewerb den ersten Preis für ein AiRail-Gebäude über dem Fernbahnhof des Frankfurter Flughafens. Eine ca. 800 Meter lange Plattform, gleichsam das Dach des Bahnhofs, bildet die Grundfläche für den 65 Meter breiten und 35 Meter hohen Baukomplex, der Air und Rail, Luftverkehr und Bahn, verbinden soll und in dieser besonderen Funktion eine spezifische Symbiose eingehen wird.

Der Reisende soll vom Bahnsteig aus unmittelbar in eine elegante großzügige Flughafenatmosphäre kommen. Ihm eröffnet sich ein breites Nutzungsspektrum – von Hotel, Gastronomie, Entertainment und Shops über ein Medical Care, Fitness und Recreation Center bis hin zu Bürobereichen. Unterschiedliche Zonen, die durch unterschiedliche Nutzung gegliedert werden, gestalten den Innenbereich. Verbindendes Element ist ein glasüberdachtes Atrium, das sich teilweise über die sechs Geschosse des Gebäudes erstreckt. Die sich über dem Bahnhof erstreckende verglaste Kuppel bleibt im zentralen Innenraum des AiRails erhalten, sie trennt und verbindet den Bahnhof mit dem darüber liegenden Gebäude.

Erschlossen wird der Bau über eine nördliche und eine südliche Vorfahrt. Zwei Parkdecks bilden den Sockel für einen geräumigen Platz, sie sind über großzügige Verbindungen an die Plaza angebunden. Mittels einer Überführung gelangt der Reisende vom Bahnhof in Ebene 03 zum nahegelegenen Terminal 1 des Flughafens.

In 1999 J•S•K won the first prize in a combined investor and architectural competition for their concept for an AiRail terminal building for the railway station at the Frankfurt airport. A approx. 800-metre long platform, similar to the roof of the railway station, forms the foundation for the 65-metre wide and 35-metre high building structure. The AiRail station forms an important link between the air and rail transportation systems, promoting a relationship of interdependence and mutual advantage.

Passengers leaving the train platform pass directly into an elegant and spacious airport atmosphere. This area opens onto a broad spectrum of facilities – from hotels, restaurants, entertainment centres and shops to a medical care, fitness and recreation centre and office areas. Various different zones, which are divided up into different spheres of utility, characterise the interior. A connecting element is provided by the atrium with its glass roof, parts of which are as high as the sixth floor of the building. The glass dome extending over the railway station continues in the main area of the AiRail terminal, connecting the railway station to the building above it. The station is serviced by two access roads: one northbound and one southbound. Two park decks form the fundament for a spacious plaza, which can be reached via generous walkways. A bridge leads passengers from the railway station on Level 03 to the nearby Terminal 1 of the airport.

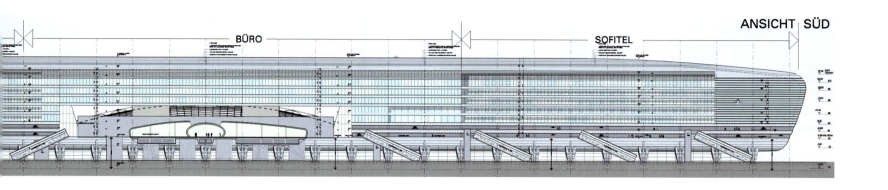

ANSICHT SÜD

BÜRO   SOFITEL

Flughafen Frankfurt am Main, AiRail

Animation Bahnhofshalle
Übersichtsplattform
Animation Grünraum

Schnitt Bahnankunft
Modell

Animation of railway station hall
Viewing platform
Animation of atrium

Cross-section rail platform
Model

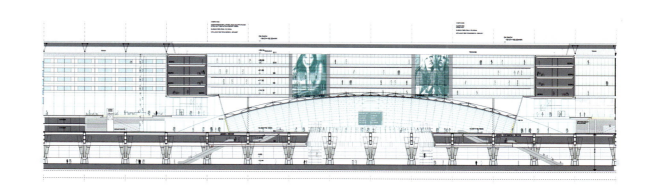

J•S•K und Perkins & Will beteiligten sich 1991 mit einem gemeinsamen Beitrag am internationalen Wettbewerb für den neuen Hongkonger Flughafen, auf dem bis zu 80 Millionen Passagiere jährlich abgefertigt werden sollen. Erschwert wurde die Aufgabe durch das vorgegebene Terrain. Der Flughafen liegt auf aufgeschüttetem Land. Es mußten daher parallel zum Terminal Start- und Landebahn positioniert werden. Der Entwurf, der bis in die letzte Entscheidungsrunde kam, kombiniert die Vorteile eines klassischen Piermodells mit denen eines Satellitenkomplexes. So konnten 120 Gatepositionen und 55 weitere auf dem Vorfeld geschaffen werden.

Auf der Ankunftsebene 01, auf der sich auch die Gepäckausgabe befinden sollte, wurde ein Bahnhof in das Terminal integriert. Darüber waren auf Ebene 02 die Check-In-Halle und die Wartebereiche an den Gates vorgesehen. Für den Individualverkehr war eine Zweiebenenvorfahrt geplant, ein People Mover sollte die Reisenden von Ebene 0 aus vom Y-förmigen Pier zum X-förmigen Satelliten bringen.

Luftseitig schließt der Entwurf an den langgestreckten repräsentativen Hauptbau mit seinem geschwungenen Dach, das die Linien der nahegelegenen Berge nachzeichnet, ein Y-förmiges Piersystem an, das lotrecht von dessen Zentrum ausgeht. Die Kreuzungspunkte des Piers werden durch Rotunden besonders hervorgehoben.

In 1991 J•S•K and Perkins & Will entered a joint concept in an international competition for the development of the new Hong Kong Airport, which was to handle an annual capacity of up to 80 million passengers. The terrain made the task especially difficult: the airport is situated on a land fill site. For this reason the runways had to be positioned parallel to the terminal. The concept, which made it to the final round of judging, combined the advantages of a classic pier model with the benefits of a satellite terminal complex. This allowed for 120 gate areas and 55 further aircraft positions to be created on the terminal apron.

On Arrivals Level 01, where the baggage claim hall was also situated, a railway station was integrated in the terminal. Above this, on Level 02, were the check-in hall and waiting lounges in the gate area. A bi-level road access system was planned for private passenger vehicles, and a People Mover would transfer passengers from the Y-shaped pier to the X-shaped satellite terminals on Level 0.

On the airside, the concept included an impressive elongated main terminal with a curved roof that reflected the line of the nearby mountains, with a Y-shaped pier system positioned perpendicular to this building. The crossing points of the pier were highlighted by rotundas.

DER FLUGHAFEN IN DI   SCHEMA BAUABSCHNITTE

1992 nahm J•S•K an einem sog. eingeladenen internationalen Wettbewerb für die Erweiterung des Flughafens Köln-Bonn teil. Es ging darum, die vorhandene Struktur des alten Flughafens durch einen neuen Pier mit Gatepositionen sowie zusätzlichen Parkmöglichkeiten zu erweitern. Der von J•S•K eingereichte, mit dem zweiten Platz ausgezeichnete Entwurf sah in einem ersten, bis 2000 fertigzustellenden Bauabschnitt eine Erhöhung der Kapazität um 7,5 Millionen Passagiere jährlich vor. In einem zweiten Bauabschnitt bis 2005 sollten die Möglichkeiten auf 12 und in einem dritten bis 2010 auf 17 Millionen Fluggäste pro Jahr weiter erhöht werden. Für das neue Terminal waren an Nettofläche 51.000 m² vorgesehen – mit 35 Positionen am Gebäude, die flexibel auf unterschiedliche Flugzeuggrößen abgestimmt werden konnten, und 50 weiteren auf dem Vorfeld. Das neue Gebäude sollte für die Reisenden und ihr Gepäck kurze Wege gewährleisten und direkte Anbindungen an den unterirdisch gelegenen Fernbahnhof sowie an S-Bahn und Bus ermöglichen.

Der Entwurf ergänzte das bestehende hufeisenförmige Gebäude des Flughafens um einen langgestreckten Gebäuderiegel in Nord-Süd-Richtung, an dem die linear aufgestellten Flugzeuge stehen sollten. Er folgt der Logik von Ankunft und Abfahrt, die an getrennte Vorfahrten auf zwei Ebenen angebunden sind. Die Mittelachse des Neubaus stellt eine Verbindung zu dem alten Flughafengebäude her und führt direkt in dessen Zentrum.

Über der Tiefgarage in Ebene 0 des neuen Terminals ist die Ankunftsebene 01 mit Zoll und Gepäckausgabe mit acht Gepäckbändern plaziert, während Abflugs- und Gatebereiche mit Check-In und Sicherheitskontrolle darüber auf Ebene 02 liegen. Die Wartezonen vor den Gates können nach Bedarf zusammengeschaltet werden. Den Abschluß nach oben bildet eine Einkaufs- bzw. Restaurantebene. Das Terminal ist schrittweise erweiterbar.

Transparenz, Weite und Leichtigkeit bestimmen die architektonische Gestalt des neuen Terminals, das sich damit auffallend vom bestehenden Bau abhebt. Deckenöffnungen und Glasfassaden lassen Ausblicke auf das angrenzende Naturschutzgebiet zu, stellen Beziehungen zwischen innen und außen her. Sie schaffen eine helle und freundliche Atmosphäre und sollen die Orientierung im Gebäude erleichtern.

In an international competition in 1992, J•S•K submitted on invitation a design concept for the expansion of Cologne-Bonn Airport. The project was to expand the existing structure of the old airport by building a new pier with additional gate areas as well as additional parking facilities. The design concept submitted by J•S•K, which was awarded second prize, encompassed an initial phase of construction, to be completed by 2000, for increasing handling capacity by 7.5 million passengers annually. In a second phase of construction, to be completed by 2005, handling capacity would be increased to 12 million passengers and in a third and final phase capacity would be increased to 17 million passengers by 2010. A net area space of 51,000 m² was planned for the new terminal – with 35 flexible docking positions for accommodating various different sizes of aircraft and an additional 50 positions on the terminal apron. The new building was designed to shorten walking distances for passengers and their luggage and to provide a direct link to the underground railway station for long-distance trains, as well as commuter trains and buses.

The concept extended the existing horseshoe-shaped building of the airport, adding an elongated arm running from north to south, along which linear-positioned aircraft would dock. It followed the logic of Arrivals and Departures, which are connected with separate access roads on two levels. The central axis of the new building provided a link to the old airport building and led directly to its centre.

Above the underground parking garage on Level 0 of the new terminal, Arrivals Level 01 with customs and the baggage claim hall with its eight baggage carousels was located. Departures with gate areas, check-in counters and security control was situated above this on Level 02. If necessary, the waiting areas in the gate area could be put together. The facilities were completed by a shopping level with restaurants and snack bars. The concept allowed for further step-by-step expansion of the terminal as required.

Transparency, space and lightness would characterise the architectural design of the new terminal, therefore making it clearly distinguishable from the other structures. Open ceilings and glass façades would allow for a good view of the neighbouring nature conservation area, creating a connection between interior and exterior. There would be a bright and friendly atmosphere with easy orientation inside the building.

58

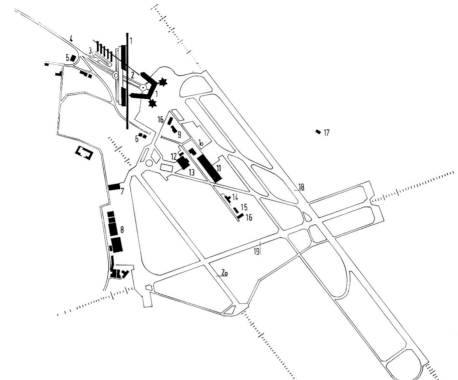

Lageplan mit Erweiterung
Erweiterung von der Luftseite

Blick auf Parkhäuser

Ground plan with extension
Extension from the airside

View of parking garages

Flughafen Köln-Bonn

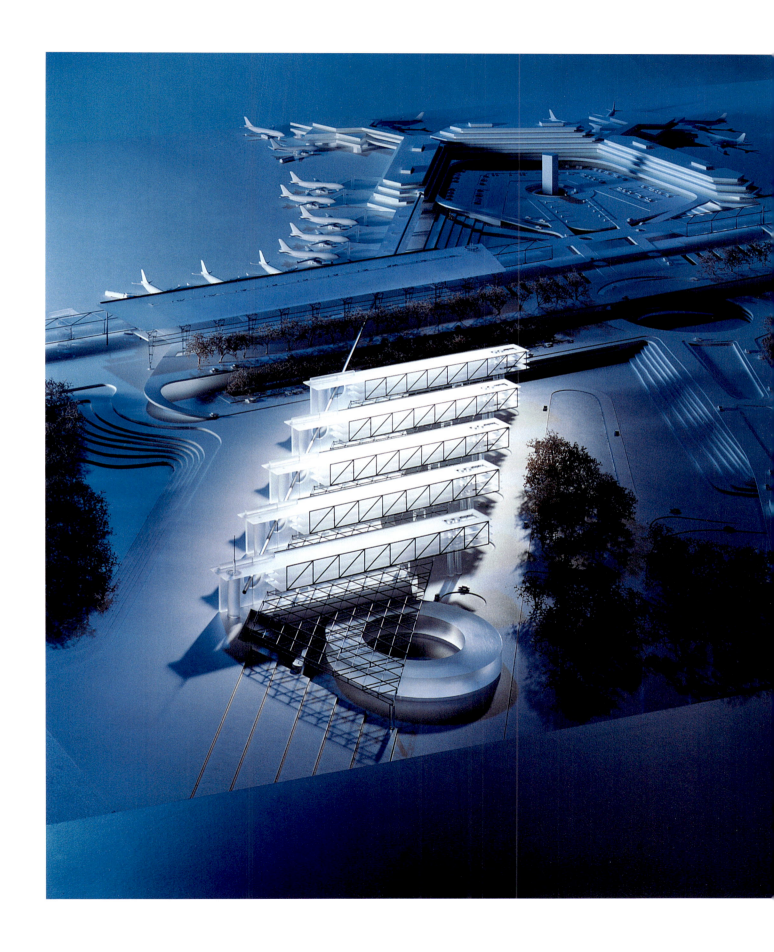

Athens International Airport
Eleftherios Venizelos, Griechenland

Zwischen 1989 bis 2000 wurde der Athener Flughafen Eleftherios Venizelos für nationale und internationale Flüge errichtet. Nach dieser ersten Ausbaustufe kann ein Aufkommen von 16 Millionen Fluggästen pro Jahr bewältigt werden. Auf geschichtsträchtigem Boden geplant, mußten ihm Berge und eine Kirche weichen, die an anderer Stelle wiederrichtet wurde. Archäologische Grabungen auf dem für den Flughafen bestimmten Areal brachten vor der Überbauung noch zahlreiche antike Funde zum Vorschein.

Die Grundkonzeption des neuen Flughafens geht von einem Satellitensystem mit einem Hauptterminal aus. In mehreren Stufen soll die Kapazität schrittweise über den Bau weiterer Satelliten auf 35 Millionen Passagiere gesteigert werden.

Der Masterplan wurde von Airconsult des Frankfurter Flughafens entwickelt. Auf der Grundlage des Masterplans des Frankfurter Flughafens erarbeitete J•S•K für HOCHTIEF das Konzept für ein Terminal mit landseitiger Erschließung und luftseitiger Andockung für 13 Positionen am Gebäude und 23 auf dem Vorfeld. Das Terminal, das beidseitig von Anbauten flankiert wird, setzt sich aus fünf hintereinander gereihten Modulen zusammen, von denen jedes seine eigene zentrale Achse besitzt, die auf der Vorfahrtseite jeweils durch einen turmartigen Bauteil gekennzeichnet wird, der sich von der übrigen Fassade abhebt und das Gebäude überragt.

HOCHTIEF hatte den Entwurf von J•S•K nach Kostengesichtspunkten überarbeitet und die internationale Ausschreibung für den Bau des Terminals und eines Satelliten mit dem zusammengeschmolzenen Konzept gewonnen. J•S•K übernahm in der Planungsphase die Detailplanung und teilweise Entwurfsplanung für die Ancillary Buildings und den Tower mit dem ATC-Building, das sich durch sein zum Turm hin ansteigendes Dach auszeichnet.

Für die Planung des Terminals hat J•S•K gestalterische Hinweise gegeben. Im realisierten Bau ist für einen unterirdischen PTS-Bahnhof vorgerüstet. Das Terminal hat eine Zweiebenenvorfahrt, an welche die Ankunftsbereiche und die Check-In-Halle angeschlossen sind. Die Teilung in Schengen- und Non-Schengen-Passagiere erfolgt durch eine horizontale Teilung im Gatebereich. Hinter den Check-In-Schaltern befindet sich eine öffentlich zugängliche Einkaufspassage. Die ein bis zweigeschossigen Bürotrakte darüber in den Achsen der fünf Module betonen die Dachlandschaft.

Der neue Athener Flughafen Eleftherios Venizelos ist weitestgehend privatwirtschaftlich finanziert, und auch der Betrieb des Flughafens erfolgt nach den gleichen Prinzipien.

Between 1989 and 2000 Athens Eleftherios Airport for domestic and international flights was built. This initial construction phase has made it possible to handle 16 million passengers per year. Planned on a historical site, it was necessary to move some small mountains and a church – which was re-erected at a different location. Archaeological diggings on the site allocated for the airport had produced numerous ancient finds before the airport was built.

The basic concept for the new airport is based on a satellite system with a main terminal. Additional satellite terminals are to be built in several phases, increasing the handling capacity of the airport to 35 million passengers annually.

The master plan was developed by the Airconsult office of Frankfurt Airport. On the basis of Frankfurt Airport's master plan, J•S•K prepared a design concept for HOCHTIEF for a terminal with access to landside transportation and airside docking with 13 gates at the building and another 23 positions on the apron. The terminal, which is flanked on both sides by adjacent buildings, consists of a row of five modules, each with its own central axis, and each of which is adorned at the front entrance with a pillar-like element that stands out distinctly from the façade and is slightly taller than the building itself.

HOCHTIEF re-worked the draft from J•S•K in terms of costs and this combined concept won the international bid for the construction of the terminal and a satellite terminal. During the planning phase, J•S•K handled the planning of all the fine points as well as some of the plans for the ancillary buildings and the control tower with the ATC building, which is characterised by a roof tapering up towards the control tower.

J•S•K also provided design consulting for the planning of the terminal. The completed building includes the basic framework for an underground People Transfer System (PTS) terminal. The terminal has a bi-level road transportation system with direct access to Arrivals and the check-in concourse. Schengen and non-Schengen passengers are separated by a horizontal division in the gate area. Behind the check-in counters is a shopping arcade with free access for the public. The one- to two-storey office complex above this, located in the axis of the five modules, characterises the design of the upper area.

The construction of the new Eleftherios Venizelos Athens Airport was financed primarily through private-sector investors, as is the operation of the airport itself.

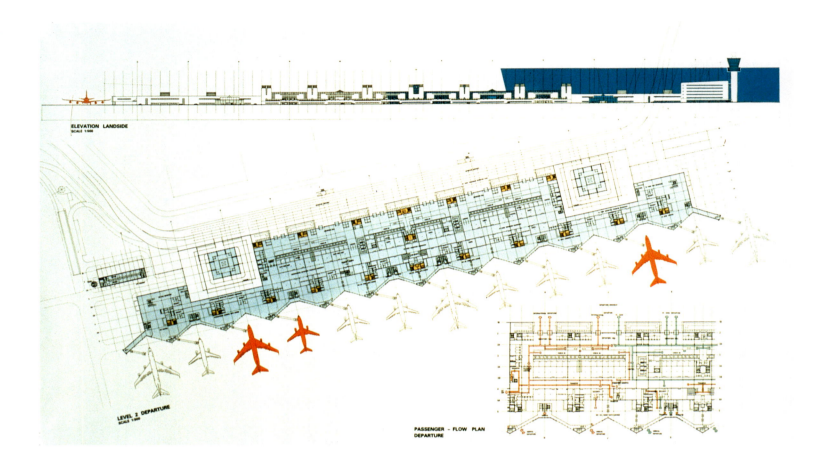

ELEVATION LANDSIDE
SCALE 1:500

LEVEL 2 DEPARTURE
SCALE 1:500

PASSENGER – FLOW PLAN
DEPARTURE

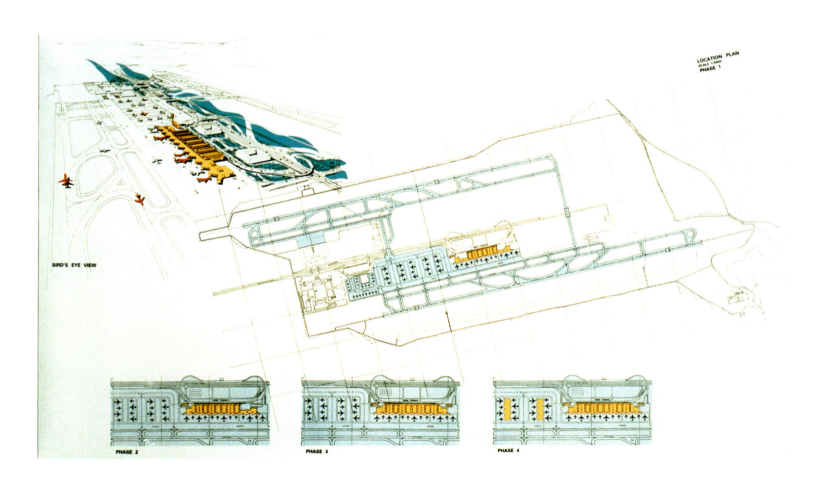

BIRD'S EYE VIEW

LOCATION PLAN
SCALE 1:5000
PHASE 1

PHASE 2

PHASE 3

PHASE 4

Athens International Airport

Ansicht Terminal mit Vorfeld

Competition concept by
  J•S•K and HOCHTIEF

View of terminal with apron

Fluggaststege
Perspektive Vorfahrt
Runway Terminal

Check-In-Schalter mit Airlinebüros
Check-In-Halle
Übersicht Check-In-Abfertigungshalle

Passenger walkways
Perspective of access road
Runway terminal

Check-in counters with airline offices
Check-in hall
View of check-in hall

Athens International Airport

Vorfahrt
Vorfahrt, Tower und ATC Building

Tower und Satellit
Nachtaufnahme Tower und ATC Building

Access roads
Access road, tower and ATC building

Tower and satellite
Night photo of tower and ATC building

Athens International Airport

Police Station und
 Maintenance Building
Archäologische Ausgrabung und Umset-
 zung einer Kirche

Building und Grounds Maintenance
Ankunft, Vorfeld und Satellit

*Police station and
 maintenance building
Archaeological dig and re-location of
 church*

*Building and grounds maintenance
Arrivals, terminal apron and satellite*

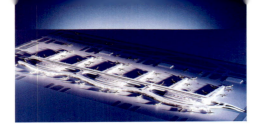

Shanghai Pu Dong International Airport, Shanghai, China

In Anbetracht des raschen wirtschaftlichen Wachstums Shanghais und der Region wurde hier ein Flughafen geplant, der stufenweise für stetig ansteigende Passagierzahlen ausgebaut und in der Zukunft 75 Millionen Fluggäste jährlich abfertigen kann. Am internationalen Wettbewerb von 1996 nahm J•S•K in Zusammenarbeit mit dem Büro Obermeyer München teil. Ihr Entwurf ging von einem Terminalmodul aus, das 25 Millionen Passagiere pro Jahr bedienen kann. Drei solcher Module hintereinander gereiht hätten bei 114 Gate- und 48 Vorfeldpositionen über die anvisierten Kapazitäten verfügt. Ein unterirdisch angelegter S-Bahnhof sollte eine schnelle Verbindung mit Shanghai ermöglichen. Jeder der Terminals für 25 Millionen Passagiere pro Jahr war nochmals in einen nationalen und einen internationalen Bereich unter einem gemeinsamen Dach geteilt.

Unter der Abflugsebene 03 mit den Wartebereichen, Sicherheitszonen und Verkaufsständen sind zwei Parkgeschosse konzipiert. Darüber – auf der Höhe der Zweiebenenvorfahrten – sind die Gepäckausgabe, Paß- und Zollkontrolle auf Ebene 04 und die Check-In-Halle mit Countern und Airlinebüros auf 05 angesiedelt. Die Vorfahrten befinden sich sowohl vor dem nationalen als auch vor dem internationalen Teil des Terminals.

Die Positionen für die Flugzeuge sind bei jedem Modul auf beiden Seiten vorgesehen, strikt getrennt in einen nationalen Bereich mit jeweils zwei Fingern für Gebäudepositionen auf der einen und einem gerundeten Gebäudeteil für internationale Flüge auf der anderen Seite. Dies entspricht den besonderen Vorschriften für chinesische Flughäfen. Ohne Kontrolle und entsprechende Ausweise ist es hier nicht möglich, zwischen dem nationalen und internationalen Bereich zu wechseln.

Mit der gewölbten gläsernen Dachform der Terminals kontrastieren die flachen Überdachungen der Flugsteige. Mit der dem Konzept innewohnenden Wiederholung gleicher Bauelemente sollten künftige Erweiterungen erleichtert werden, die einzelnen Elemente verbinden sich zu einer harmonischen Gesamtform.

In view of the rapid economic growth in Shanghai and the surrounding region, an airport was planned here that can be gradually expanded to accommodate the steadily rising number of passengers and that will, in the future, be able to handle 75 million passengers a year. In collaboration with Obermeyer Munich, J•S•K took part in an international competition for the development of Shanghai International in 1996. Their design concept was based on a terminal module that would be able to serve 25 million passengers annually. Three such modules organised in a row, with a total of 114 gates and 48 terminal apron positions would provide the targeted capacity. An underground commuter train station would offer fast connections to and from Shanghai. Each of the terminals with its annual handling capacity of 25 million passengers would be sub-divided into national and international areas, both under one common roof.

Below Departures Level 03, with its waiting lounges, security check points and shops, the concept included two parking levels. Above this – on the same levels as the bi-level road access system – were the baggage claim hall, passport and customs check points on Level 04 and a concourse area with check-in counters and airline offices on Level 05. The access roads were located along the front of both the national and the international sections of the terminal.

The docking positions for the aircraft were to be placed on either side of the module, strictly divided into a national area with two piers for docking on one side and a round building for international flights on the other. This was in accordance with the special regulations for Chinese airports. Without passing through control check points and showing the necessary identification, it is not possible to pass between the national and international areas.

The flat roofs of the piers were an interesting contrast to the dome-shaped glass roof of the terminal. In the concept, the repetitive use of the same building components would facilitate future expansion: the individual elements would be connected to form a harmonious unity.

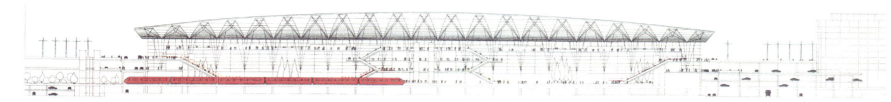

Modell Perspektive
Animation Check-In-Halle

Längsschnitt
Warteräume Finger National
Modell

Model perspective
Animation of check-in hall

Longitudinal section
Waiting rooms, pier for domestic flights
Model

Shanghai Pu Dong International Airport

Bahnhof
Modell Modul

Übersichtsplan
Finger National

Railway station
Model of module

Layout plan
Pier for domestic flights

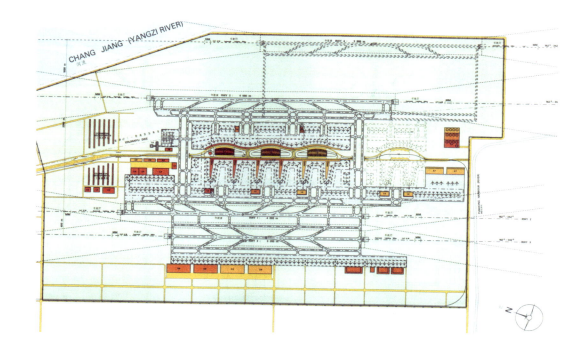

Flughafen Münster-Osnabrück

Zwischen 1993 bis 1995 wurde der Flughafen Münster-Osnabrück auf der Grundlage eines Wettbewerbsbeitrags ausgebaut, für den J•S•K 1990 der erste Preis zugesprochen worden war. Wesentliche Gestaltungselemente der Bestandsarchitektur wurden in das Erweiterungskonzept transformiert und beide Bauteile zu einer formalen und funktionalen Einheit zusammengeschlossen.

Das neue Terminalgebäude von 150 Metern Länge und 70 Metern Breite verfügt über drei Ebenen. Die Abflughalle mit Check-In-Schaltern, Sicherheitskontrolle und Wartezonen sowie der Ankunftsbereich mit Gepäckausgabe und Zollkontrolle befinden sich auf dem gleichen Niveau, an das auch die Vorfahrt angeschlossen ist. Über der Check-In-Halle liegen eine Galerie, Wartebereiche, Restaurant- und Büroflächen. Zwei Gebäudepositionen und zwei weitere auf dem Vorfeld erlauben die Abfertigung von insgesamt max. 10 Millionen Passagieren jährlich. Als Zwischenglied und Verbindung zum bestehenden Flughafengebäude wurde ein Bürobereich für die Flughafenverwaltung geplant.

Bei Bedarf kann das linear strukturierte Ensemble um eine Achse nach Westen und mehrere Achsen nach Osten erweitert werden, ohne seinen gestalterischen und funktionalen Ausdruck zu verlieren.

Der 'im Grünen' gelegene Flughafen soll im Einklang mit der Natur stehen. Von einer großzügigen Grün- und Landschaftsgestaltung umgeben, wird er harmonisch in die umliegende Heidelandschaft eingebettet. Die Transparenz der flachen Dächer wie der Fassaden macht den Naturraum erlebbar und führt zu transparenten Innenräumen, die optisch und gedanklich die Land- und Luftseite miteinander verbinden. Die leichte gläserne Raumhülle und die filigrane Stahlkonstruktion sowie die ausgewählten Materialien und die großzügige Verbindung der Ankunfts- und Abflugbereiche machen das Terminal übersichtlich und sympathisch.

Between 1993 and 1995 Münster-Osnabrück Airport was enlarged on the basis of the design concept for which J•S•K had won first prize in a competition in 1990. Basic design elements of the existing architecture were transformed in the development process and both sections of the building were connected to create a unified structure in terms of design and function.

The new terminal building, 150 metres in length and 70 metres across, has three levels. The departures area, with its check-in counters, security check points and waiting areas, is on the same level as the arrivals area, with the baggage claim hall and customs screening, as well as the access road. Above the check-in area are a gallery, waiting lounges, restaurants and offices. Two gate positions plus another two aircraft positions on the terminal apron make it possible to handle of a total capacity of no more than 10 million passengers a year. As a connecting link to the existing terminal building, an office area for the airport administration was planned.

If necessary, the linear structure can later be expanded by one axis to the west and several more to the east, without altering the design or affecting functionality.

The airport is intended to blend in with nature through its 'out in the country' location. Surrounded by a generous zone of natural landscaping, it blends in harmoniously with the surrounding heathland. The transparency of the flat roof and walls makes it possible for passengers to experience the natural settings from inside the building, while creating transparent interior spaces that optically and stylistically connect the land- and airsides of the airport. The light glass walls and ceilings of the building and the intricate steel construction, as well as the carefully selected materials and the spacious concourse area between Arrivals and Departures, give the terminal a clear-cut and attractive appearance.

Oberlicht Bürotrakt

Lageplan
Perspektive Vorfahrtseite
Modell Luftseite

Skylight in office block

Ground plan
Perspective of access road side
Model of airside

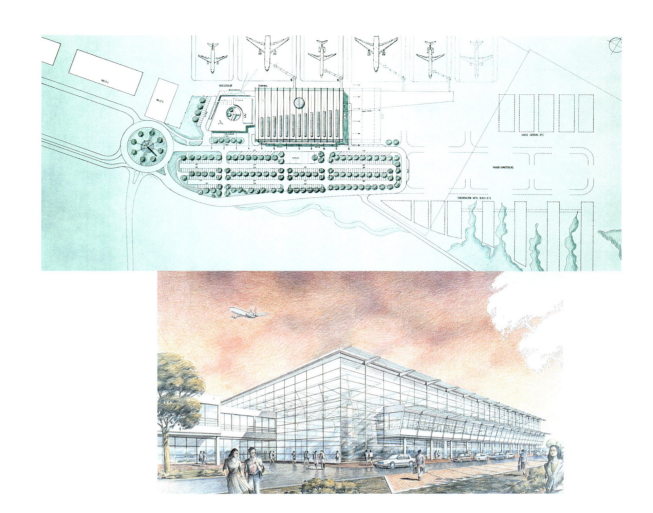

Eingang Vorfahrt
Grundriß Erweiterung und Ansichten

Fassade der Vorfahrt

Entrance on access road side
Floor plan of extension and overview

Façade on access road side

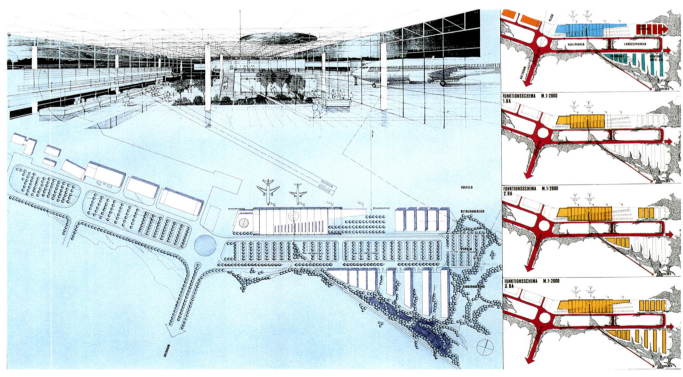

Flughafen Münster-Osnabrück

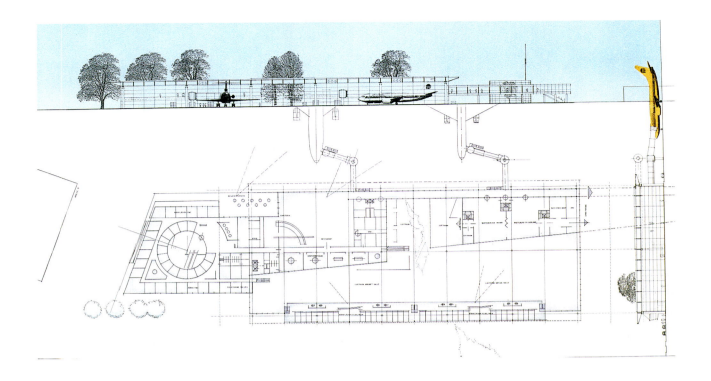

Flughafen Münster-Osnabrück

Grundriß Check-In Halle
Check-In-Halle

Fassade mit Vorfahrt
Blick vom Vorfeld in Check-In-Halle

Floor plan of check-in hall
Check-in hall

Façade and access road
View from the apron into check-in hall

Vorfeld mit Flugsteig

Blick im Flugsteig zum Terminal
Seitenansicht bei Nacht

Terminal apron with pier

View in pier of terminal
Side view at night

Flughafen Münster-Osnabrück

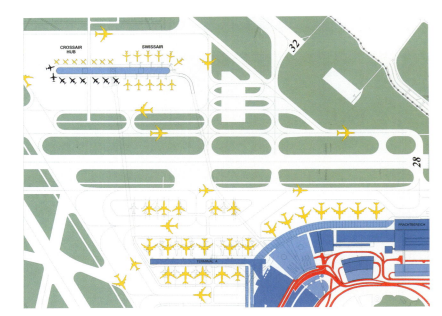

1997 erstellte J•S•K für den Flughafen Zürich ein Gutachten, das Planungen für ein weiteres drittes Terminal sowie einen Satelliten beinhaltete, welche die Abfertigung von 15 Millionen Passagieren im Jahr ermöglichen sollten. Für beide Bauten wurden Standorte zwischen dem Terminal A und dem Verwaltungsgebäude der Fluggesellschaft Swiss Air gewählt. Der neue Terminalbau mit landseitiger Zweiebenenerschliessung und luftseitig acht Gebäudepositionen, der den Reisenden und ihrem Gepäck kurze Wege gewährleisten sollte, war mit einem Untergeschoß für die Gepäcksortierung und die dazugehörigen Technikräumen geplant. Auf Ebene 0 darüber lag neben Gewerbeflächen für Konzessionäre die Vorfahrt mit einer Verbindung zur Ankunftsebene 1, die wiederum an den Pier auf der Luftseite angeschlossen war. Auf der Ankunftsebene mit Pieranbindung befanden sich die Gepäckausgabe und die Ankunftshalle. Ebene 2 sollte für den Abflug bestimmt bleiben. Neben der Check-In-Halle mit ca. 50 Countern, den Wartezonen, Lounges und den Bordkarten-, Paß- und Sicherheitskontrollen für die abfliegenden Passagiere waren hier aber auch Läden und Restaurants für Flug- und andere Gäste vorgesehen. Am Satelliten wurden weitere 22 Gatepositionen geplant.

Die Idee war, die vorhandenen Terminals A und B durch ein drittes Terminal zu ergänzen, ein Versuch, die Kapazitäten des Flughafens auszunutzen, bevor ein Ausbau mit einem Satelliten notwendig wurde.

In 1997 J•S•K prepared an expert report for the development of Zurich Airport, which included plans for a further, third terminal as well as a satellite terminal, which would make it possible to handle 15 million passengers a year. As a location for both structures, the space between Terminal A and the Swiss Air administration building was chosen.
The new terminal building with a bi-level road access system and eight docking positions on the terminal apron, guaranteed to shorten walking distances for passengers with their luggage, was planned with a basement area for baggage sorting and the necessary rooms for technical equipment. On Level 0 above this were commercial space for concessions and the access road with a direct link to Arrivals Level 1, which itself was directly connected to the pier on the airside. On the arrivals level, in addition to the arrivals area with access to the gate areas, was the baggage claim hall. Level 2 was to be reserved for the departures area. In addition to the check-in hall with approx. 50 counters, the waiting areas, lounges and the check points for boarding tickets, passports and security for departing passengers, the concept also included plans for shops and restaurants for both passengers and non-passengers. Another 22 gate areas were planned at the satellite terminal.
The idea was to supplement the existing Terminals A and B with a third terminal, in an attempt to increase the handling capacity of the airport before it became necessary to add a satellite terminal.

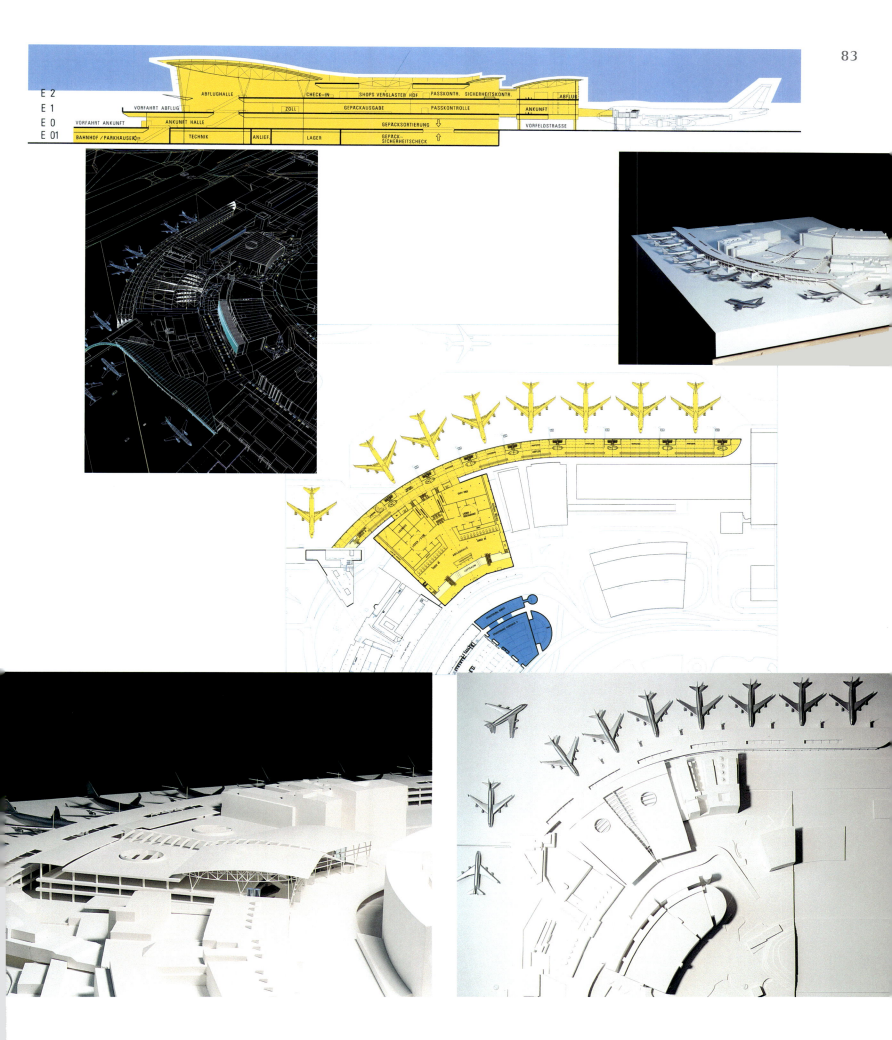

E 2
E 1
E 0
E 01

VORFAHRT ABFLUG
VORFAHRT ANKUNFT
ANKUNFT HALLE
BAHNHOF / PARKHÄUSER

ABFLUGHALLE
CHECK-IN
SHOPS VERGLASTER HOF
PASSKONTR. SICHERHEITSKONTR.
ABFLUG

ZOLL
GEPÄCKAUSGABE
PASSKONTROLLE
ANKUNFT

GEPÄCKSORTIERUNG
VORFELDSTRASSE

TECHNIK
ANLIEF.
LAGER
GEPÄCK-
SICHERHEITSCHECK

1996 wurde der drittgrößte deutsche Flughafen durch einen Brand schwer beschädigt. Dieses Ereignis gab den Anlaß für grundsätzlichere Überlegungen zu einer Neugestaltung und Vergrößerung der Anlage über eine Sanierung der betroffenen Bauten hinaus. Aus dem internationalen Wettbewerb „airport 2000 plus" ging der Entwurf des Büros J•S•K im Januar 1997 als Sieger hervor. Das Projekt zeichnete sich nicht zuletzt durch sein land- wie luftseitig großes Erweiterungspotential aus, das in mehreren Stufen verwirklicht werden kann.

Wesentlicher Bestandteil der Umgestaltung und Neustrukturierung des Düsseldorfer Flughafens ist die Integration der vorhandenen Abfertigungsbauten in ein zukunftsträchtiges Gesamtkonzept. Die in ihrer Form und Länge unterschiedlichen Flugsteige A, B und C und Teile des Zentralgebäudes werden landseitig durch ein erweiterbares halbkreisförmiges Terminal in eine einheitliche, organische Gesamtarchitektur gegliedert. In einem zweiten Bauabschnitt wird diese Struktur gegenläufig fortgesetzt. Die Entwicklung folgt damit einer S-förmigen Linie, an der entlang die einzelnen Teile und Funktionen additiv aneinandergereiht werden können. Dieses modulare Konzept erlaubt eine hohe Flexibilität.

Die Planungen gehen von einer jährlichen Abfertigung von zunächst 17 und nach dem zweiten Bauabschnitt von maximal 22 Millionen Passagieren und 43 Gatepositionen aus. Mit der Realisierung wurde im März 1997 begonnen. Folgende Baumaßnahmen wurden bis zum Frühjahr 2001 neben der Modernisierung und Sanierung des Bestands abgeschlossen: die Umgestaltung von Flugsteig A, die Sanierung des Flugsteigs C, der Abriß und Neubau von Flugsteig B, die Erweiterung und der Neubau des Zentralgebäudes, der Bau einer Tiefgarage im Untergeschoß mit einer neuen Vorfahrtsplatte sowie die Realisierung eines People Mover Systems (PM), das einen neuen Fernbahnhof mit dem neugestalteten Terminal verbinden soll. Im Anschluß an diese Baumaßnahmen ist die Verlängerung der zentralen Halle im Bereich Flugsteig C vorgesehen. Nach Vollendung des ersten Bauabschnitts wird das halbkreisförmige, ca. 80 Meter breite Terminal die drei Flugsteige über eine Länge von 400 Metern verbinden.

Die geschwungene Großform der Gesamtanlage gibt dem Flughafen eine unverwechselbare Architektur. Ein innovatives Konzept wird konsequent umgesetzt.

In 1996 the third-largest German airport, Düsseldorf International, was extensively damaged by fire. The subsequent repair measures provided the opportunity for more basic considerations for rebuilding and enlarging the airport at the same time. The winner of the international "Airport 2000 plus" competition in January 1997 was the design concept submitted by J•S•K. The project was characterised not least by its immense potential for expansion, both landside and airside, which could be realised in several phases of development.

An essential component of the redesigning and restructuring of Düsseldorf International was the integration of existing terminal sections in an overall future-oriented concept. Piers A, B and C, with their varying shapes and lengths, and parts of the main building were divided on the landside by an expandable semi-circle-shaped terminal in a unified, organic architectural structure. In a second phase of construction this unit was continued in the opposite direction. The development therefore follows an S-shaped line, to which rows of individual modules and functions can be added when necessary. This modular concept allows for a high level of flexibility.

The design concept was based on an initial phase of construction to create an annual handling capacity of 17 million passengers, and a second phase to create a maximum capacity of 22 million, with 43 gate positions. Building commenced in March 1997. The following building measures were to be completed by the spring 2001, in addition to the modernisation and renovation of the existing building: reconstruction of Pier A, renovation of Pier C, demolishing and rebuilding of Pier B, expansion and rebuilding of the main terminal building, construction of a parking garage on the lower level with a new access road as well as the realisation of a People Mover system (PM) that would connect the new railway station for long-distance trains to the newly-designed terminal building. After completion of these building measures there were plans for the extension of the main concourse in the area of Pier C. After completion of the first phase of construction the semicircle-shaped, approx. 80-metre wide terminal would connect the three piers along a length of 400 metres.

The generous curved shape of the overall construction lends the airport an unmistakable architecture: an innovative concept implemented true to form.

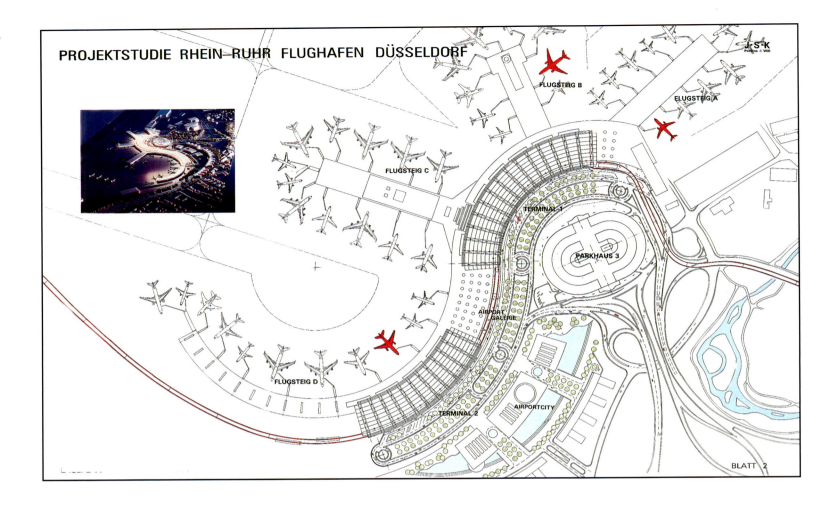

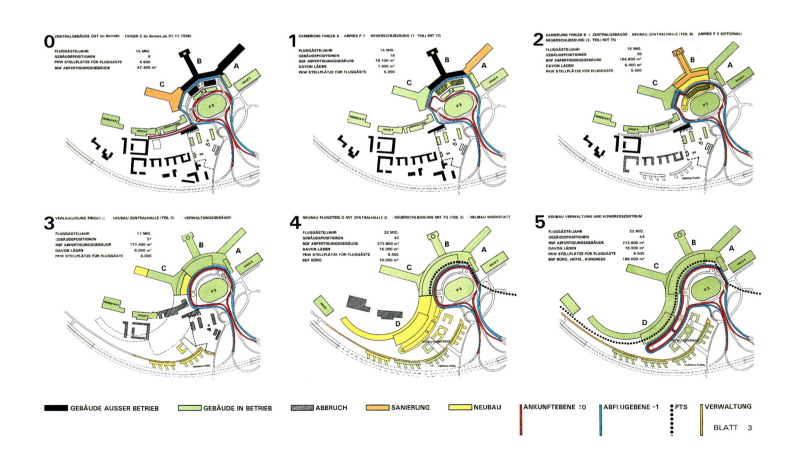

Lageplan
Bauphasenplan

Luftbild

Ground plan
Development phase plan

Aerial photo

Flughafen Düsseldorf International, Zentralgebäude

Im Juni 2001 war die 1997 begonnene Umgestaltung und landseitige Vergrößerung des Zentralgebäudes des Düsseldorfer Flughafens abgeschlossen. Charakteristikum der neuen Architektur ist die markant geschwungene Dachkonstruktion, deren elliptisches Profil im Bereich der Vorfahrt das People Mover System aufnimmt. Eine der wohl spektakulärsten Einzelbaumaßnahmen für das neue Terminal war die Montage der Dachträger, die das 12.000 m² große Hallendach tragen. Es besteht aus 16 speziell angefertigten Dreigurtbindern und Pfetten als Sekundärträgern und Trapezblech für die Dachhaut.

Die Glas-Aluminium-Fassade des Gebäudes mit ihren großen Fensterflächen bietet einen Blick auf die Vorfahrt und das Vorfeld. Das Tageslicht, das über Oberlichter im Bereich der Dachbinder einfällt, sorgt für die natürliche Belichtung der runden zentralen Halle.

Das neue Terminal verfügt über zwei Parkdecks. Auf der Ankunftsebene 0 mit der Vorfahrt und dem Zugang zum unterirdischen S-Bahnhof befinden sich neben der Gepäckausgabe in der Ankunftshalle die Information, diverse gastronomische Einrichtungen und die Schalter der Autovermietungen. Der Abflug mit den Check-In-Bereichen, den Ticket- und Sondergepäckschaltern ist auf Ebene 1 eingerichtet. Weitere vielfältige Service- und Dienstleistungsangebote ergänzen die Abflughalle. Nach dem Einchecken werden die Reisenden über Ladenpassagen und Restaurantzonen zu den Flugsteigen geführt. Auf zwei Galerieebenen über dem Abflug befinden sich ein Medical Care Center sowie ein Konferenzbereich. Eine Gebets- und Gedenkstätte für die Opfer der Brandkatastrophe von 1996 wurde hier ebenfalls eingerichtet.

Ein People Mover (PM) verbindet, mit einer Haltestation zwischen den Flugsteigen A und B, den im Jahr 2000 eröffneten Fernbahnhof des Flughafens, der nicht direkt auf dem Flughafengelände liegt. Die Verbindung des Bahnhofs mit dem Flughafen erfolgt über eine Hängebahn, welche die Rolle des People Movers übernimmt. Die Streckenführung der vollautomatischen Hängebahn (PM), die im Sommer 2002 ihren regulären Betrieb aufnehmen und dann auch einen weiteren Haltepunkt an einem der Parkhäuser haben wird, verläuft über der Vorfahrt in der elliptisch ausgebildeten Dachkonstruktion. Die formale Einbeziehung des im Dachbereich geführten PMs vollendet die wichtige Vernetzung der Verkehrssysteme Flugzeug, Bahn und Auto.

The restructuring and landside enlargement of the main terminal building of Düsseldorf International, which had commenced in 1997, was completed in June 2001. Characteristic of the new architecture is the distinctive curved roof construction, whose elliptical profile includes a People Mover system close to the access road. One of the most spectacular individual building measures involved in the new terminal was the assembly of the immense structure supporting the 12,000 m² roof of the concourse. It consists of 16 specially-constructed triangular rafters and perlins as secondary supports, with trapezoidal sheet metal for the roof covering.

The glass and aluminium façade of the building with its generous windows offers a view of the access road on the one side and the terminal apron on the other. Daylight flooding in through skylights between the rafters provides natural lighting in the circular concourse area.

The new terminal has two parking decks. On Arrivals Level 0, along with the access road and the entrance to the underground commuter train station, are the baggage claim hall in the arrivals area, an information desk, assorted restaurants and snack bars and the car rentals desk. Departures with check-in areas, ticket counters and a check-in counter for bulkier items are located on Level 1. Other assorted services and facilities complete the departures area. After checking in, the passengers walk past shops and restaurants to the gate area. On two gallery levels above the departures area are a medical care centre and a conference area. A prayer and meditation chapel for the casualties of the airport fire of 1996 has also been erected here.

A People Mover (PM) on overhead rails facilitates the movement of passengers between various sections of the airport, with a stop between Piers A and B. It also connects the airport to the railway station for long-distance trains, which was opened in the year 2000 and is not situated directly on the airport grounds. The route of the fully automated People Mover, which will begin full operations in the summer of 2002 and will then also have an additional stop at one of the parking garages, follows the access road in the elliptically shaped roof construction. The PM provides a final essential link to complete the air, rail and road transportation network.

Konstruktion Halle Bauphase
und People Mover

*Terminal under construction
and People Mover*

Detail Verkleidung People Mover
Blick in Zentralhalle

People Mover
Bahnhof People Mover

Close-up of People Mover covering
View in main concourse

People Mover
People Mover terminal

Check-In Zentralhalle
Ankunftsebene und Halle

Zentralgebäude
Zentralhalle

Main check-in hall
Arrivals level and concourse

Main terminal building
Central concourse

Flughafen Düsseldorf International, Zentralgebäude

Animation Zentralhalle
Verbindung Halle und A-Finger

Halle Zentralgebäude und Zugangsbereich
    Flugsteig B
Blick auf Zentralhalle mit Oberlicht

Animation main concourse
Connecting walkway and Pier A

Central concourse in mcin terminal and
    walkway to Pier B
View of main concourse with skylights

Flughafen Düsseldorf International, Zentralgebäude

Atrium an der Zentralhalle
Blick vom Flugsteig B in die Halle

Aufgang zum Flugsteig B

Atrium in the main concourse
View of main concourse from Pier B

Escalators to Pier B

Gleichzeitig mit den Arbeiten im Zentralbereich des Flughafens begannen auch die Rückbauarbeiten am Flugsteig B, der bis auf den Kontrollturm vollständig abgerissen und im Bereich zwischen dem Tower und der neuen Tiefgarage verbreitert und mit veränderten Geschoßhöhen wieder aufgebaut wurde. Der Tower blieb während der gesamten Baumaßnahmen in Betrieb. Der Flugsteig B wurde mit der Zentralhalle im Juni 2001 fertiggestellt.

In dem 170 Meter langen und 70 Meter breiten Gebäude befinden sich sowohl Ankunft als auch Abflug für die Schengen- und Non-Schengen-Passagiere zusammen mit den Wartebereichen, der Sicherheitskontrolle, einer Lounge und einem Restaurant auf Ebene 2. Die gleichen Einrichtungen für die Non-Schengen-Reisenden mit Sicherheits- und Paßkontrolle sind darunter auf Ebene 1 angesiedelt. Unter beiden Bereichen, auf der Vorfeldebene, liegen die zentrale Gepäcksortierung für den Flughafen Düsseldorf und einige Büros der Fluggesellschaften. Die Besucherterrasse ist an die Galerieebene 3 mit einer weiteren Lounge, Shops und gastronomischen Einrichtungen angebunden. Die Glastürme der Treppenhäuser, die sich an den Gatepositionen befinden, akzentuieren die Außensilhouette des Flugsteigs B. Der bestehende Tower ist von dem neuen B-Finger völlig umbaut worden, so daß nur noch seine Kontrollräume über diesen hinausragen.

At the same time as work commenced in the main area of the airport, reconstruction also began on Pier B, which, except for the control tower, was completely demolished and then rebuilt in the area between the control tower and the new underground parking garage, this time with a different number of levels. The control tower remained in operation during the entire construction period. Pier B and the main concourse area were completed in June 2001.

The 170-metre long and 70-metre wide building contains both Arrivals and Departures for Schengen and non-Schengen passengers as well as waiting lounges, security control, a lounge and a restaurant on Level 2. The same facilities for non-Schengen passengers with security and passport check points are located below this on Level 1. Below both of these areas, on ground level, are located the central baggage sorting for Düsseldorf International and several airlines offices. The aircraft viewing terrace is on Gallery Level 3 with access to a further lounge, shops and restaurants and snack bars. The glass towers of the staircases in the gate areas accentuate the exterior silhouette of Pier B. The existing control tower is completely surrounded by the new Pier B, so that only its control rooms extend above the building.

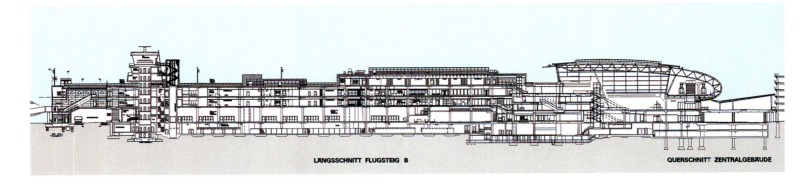

LÄNGSSCHNITT FLUGSTEIG B

QUERSCHNITT ZENTRALGEBÄUDE

Schnitt Zentralhalle und Flugsteig B
Einkaufspassage zur Halle
Aufgang zum Flugsteig B
Restaurantebene

Atrium der Zentralhalle

Section of main concourse and Pier B
Shopping arcade
Escalators to Pier B
Restaurant level

Atrium in the main concourse

Flughafen Düsseldorf International, Flugsteig B

Check-In-Schalter
Wartebereich

Blick auf den B-Finger vom Vorfeld
Verkaufsebene

Check-in counters
Waiting area

View of Pier B from the apron
Shopping level

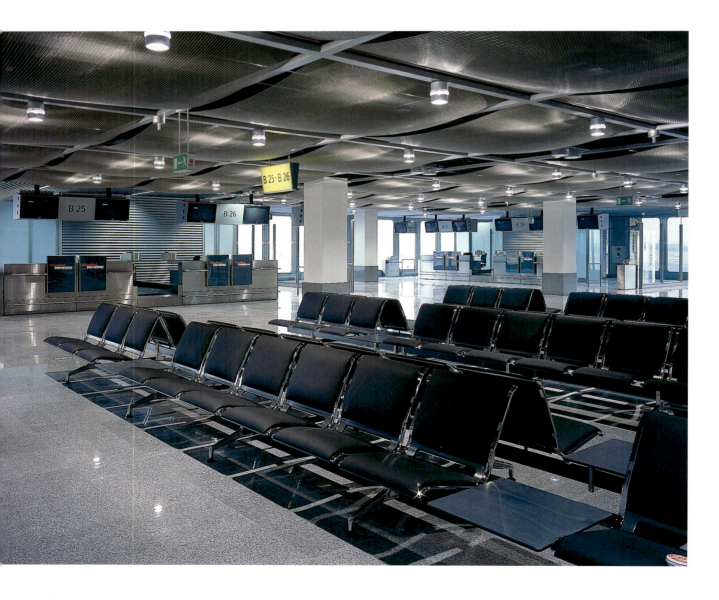

Flughafen Düsseldorf International, Flugsteig B

Fluggastbrücken und Gepäckkontrolle

Detail Treppenhäuser
Treppenhäuser

Passenger bridges and baggage control

Close-up of staircases
Staircases

Flughafen Düsseldorf International, Flugsteig B

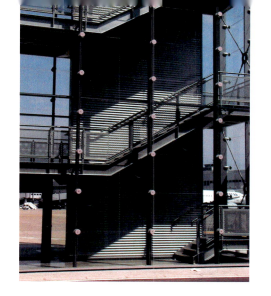

Oberlicht Ankunft Flugsteig A
Ankunftsebene

Ankunft Flugsteig A

Skylights in Arrivals Pier A
Arrivals level

Arrivals Pier A

Die Flugsteige C und A sind saniert und umgebaut worden.
Der 230 Meter lange und 45 Meter breite Finger A wurde
zwischen Januar 1997 und April 1998 komplett renoviert. Die
wesentlichen Materialien für den Gebäudeteil sind Naturstein,
Metall und Glas. Das zentrale Oberlicht betont die Hauptver-
kehrsachse des Flugsteig A, ermöglicht eine natürliche Belichtung des Gebäudes und erleichtert die Orientierung für die
Passagiere. Die verglasten Stahlbrücken verbinden die einzelnen Galerieebenen miteinander und rhythmisieren gleichzeitig den zentralen Gang.
Der Flugsteig A wird von der Lufthansa für ihre Passagiere
genutzt, die abfliegen oder ankommen. Die Trennung der
Schengen- und Non-Schengen-Passagiere erfolgt im A-Finger nicht in verschiedenen Ebenen, er ist vielmehr horizontal
geteilt. Im Endbereich des Fingers werden die internationalen
Passagiere abgefertigt.
Flugsteig C, der bei einer Breite von 50 Metern 175 Meter
lang ist, wurde unmittelbar nach dem Brand wiederhergestellt
und wurde bereits im November 1996 in Betrieb genommen.
Der Abflug und die Ankunft liegen auf der Ebene 2. Eine Galerieebene und ein Technikgeschoß bilden den Abschluß.
Aufgrund der Brandkatastrophe am Düsseldorfer Flughafen
wurde ein neues Brandschutzkonzept entwickelt, das zuerst
bei den Flugsteigen C und A angewendet wurde.

Piers A and C have now been renovated and reconstructed.
The 230-metre long and 45-metre wide Pier A was completely
rebuilt between January 1997 and April 1998. The basic ma-
terials for the building are natural stone, metal and glass. The
central skylights in the roof highlight the main traffic artery of
Pier A, flooding the building with natural light and facilitating
orientation for the passengers. Glass and steel bridges connect
the individual gallery levels and also lend a rhythmic quality
to the main concourse.
Pier A is used by Lufthansa for its passengers, both departing
and arriving. The Schengen and non-Schengen passengers in
Pier A are not separated on different levels, but rather divided
horizontally. International passengers are processed at the far
end of the pier.
With a width of 50 metres and a length of 175 metres, Pier C
was rebuilt immediately after the fire and was ready to re-
sume operations as soon as November 1996. Departures and
Arrivals are situated on Level 2. A gallery level and a separ-
ate floor for technical equipment complete the facilities.
Since the fire at Düsseldorf International, a new fire protec-
tion concept has been developed, and was first implemented
in Piers C and A.

Flughafen Düsseldorf International, Flugsteige A und C

Check-In-Wartebereich Flugsteig A
Abflugsebene Flugsteig A

Restaurant Flugsteig A
ALU Bar Flugsteig A

Check-in waiting area Pier A
Departures level Pier A

Restaurant Pier A
ALU bar Pier A

Beleuchtete Säule Flugsteig C
Zugang Flugsteig C
Ankunfsgang Flugsteig C

Zugang zur S-Bahn Flugsteig C

Illuminated pillar Pier C
Walkway Pier C
Arrival walkway Pier C

Walkway to S-Bahn Pier C

Flughafen Düsseldorf International, Flugsteige A und C

Beim internationalen Realisierungswettbewerb für das Terminal 2 des Münchener Flughafens im Jahre 1998 wurde der Beitrag von J•S•K in die zweite Ranggruppe eingestuft. Aufgabe war es, ein neues Terminal mit einem Satelliten an das Münchener Airport Centrum (MAC) anzuschließen und das bestehende Terminal mit parallel gegenüberliegenden Abfertigungsanlagen zu ergänzen.

In Zusammenarbeit mit dem Ingenieurbüro Obermeyer aus München, das die Verkehrsplanung entwickelt hatte, wurde entgegen den Planungsvorgaben für das neue Terminal eine Zweiebenenvorfahrt geplant. Sie führt an diesem vorbei und fügt sich harmonisch in das gesamte Verkehrssystem am Münchener Flughafen ein. Das Terminal orientiert sich an den linear aufgestellten Flugzeugen und ihren Gatepositionen. Geplant wurde ein zentrales Terminal mit zu diesem parallel liegendem Finger.

Ein Bahnhof wird auf der Ebene 0 integriert. 25 Gebäudegates und 22 Vorfeldpositionen ermöglichen die Abfertigung von jährlich 20 Millionen Passagieren. Die Ankunftsebene über dem Bahnhof ist für die Gepäckausgabe mit zehn Gepäckbändern sowie die Zollkontrolle für ankommende Flugreisende bestimmt. Eine großzügige lichterfüllte Passage verknüpft auf dieser Ebene das Terminal mit dem MAC Forum. Schengen- und Non-Schengen-Passagieren sind getrennte Abflugsebenen zugewiesen, auf denen neben Wartebereichen und anderen notwendigen Ausrüstungen wie der Sicherheitskontrolle auch Shops und gastronomische Einrichtungen vorgesehen sind.

In Maßstäblichkeit und Dimensionierung wie in der unaufdringlichen horizontal ausgerichteten Ausführung seines filigranen Hauptdachs, welches bewußt die expressive Dachform des MAC noch mehr hervortreten läßt, bezieht sich Terminal 2 auf die bestehenden Bauten des Münchener Flughafens. Der leicht abgesenkte, vollständig transparente Mittelbereich bildet die Verbindung zur zentralen Achse der Gesamtanlage.

In an international competition for the development of Terminal 2 of Munich Airport in the year 1998, the concept submitted by J•S•K was ranked second. The task was to add a new satellite terminal to the Munich Airport Centrum (MAC) and supplement the existing terminal with parallel processing equipment.

In collaboration with engineering consultants Obermeyer from Munich, who had developed the plans for the traffic system, a bi-level road access system was planned for the new terminal, contrary to the specifications for the concept. Traversing the terminal, this route was a harmonious supplement to the overall transportation system of Munich Airport. The terminal was oriented to the linear arrangement of the aircraft docking positions and the gate areas. Included in the concept was a central terminal with a parallel gate area.

A railway station was to be integrated on Level 0. A total of 25 gates and 22 docking positions on the terminal apron would make it possible to handle 20 million passengers a year. The arrivals level above the railway station was intended for the baggage claim hall with ten baggage carousels, as well as customs check points for arriving passengers. A spacious, light and airy corridor on this level would connect the terminal to the MAC Forum. There were separate departure levels for Schengen and non-Schengen passengers with waiting lounges and other necessary facilities such as security check points, as well as shops, restaurants and snack bars.

In terms of proportion and dimension, as well as the unobtrusive horizontal arrangement of its intricate main roof, which consciously underscores the expressive roof design of the MAC even further, Terminal 2 blends in well with the existing buildings of Munich Airport. The slightly sunken, completely transparent central concourse area forms the connecting link to the central axis of the overall structure.

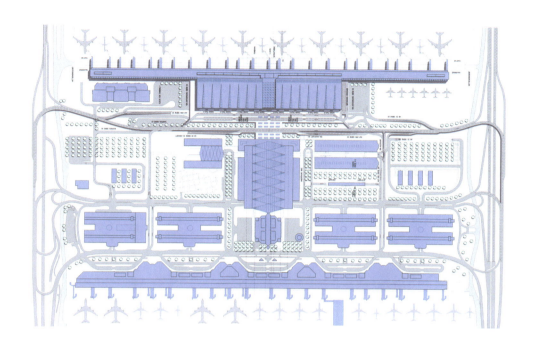

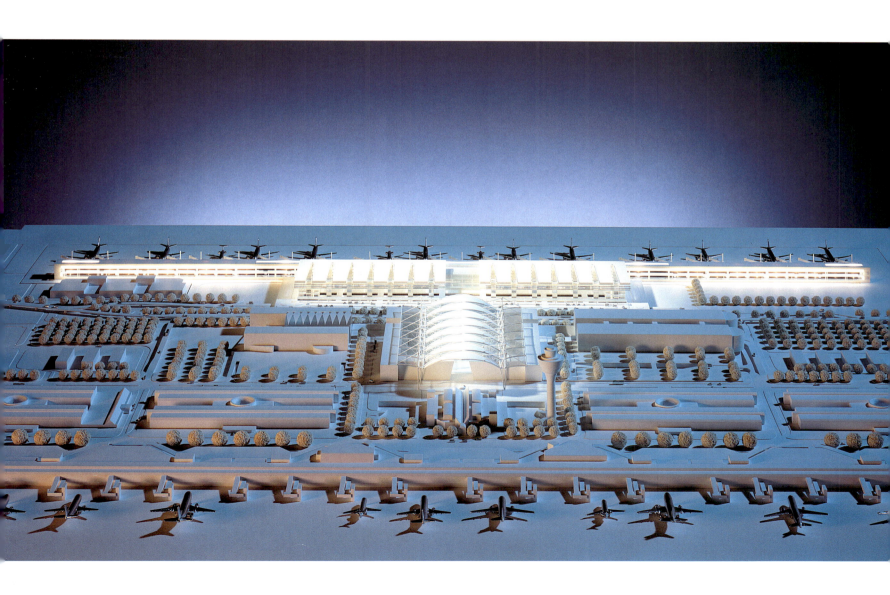

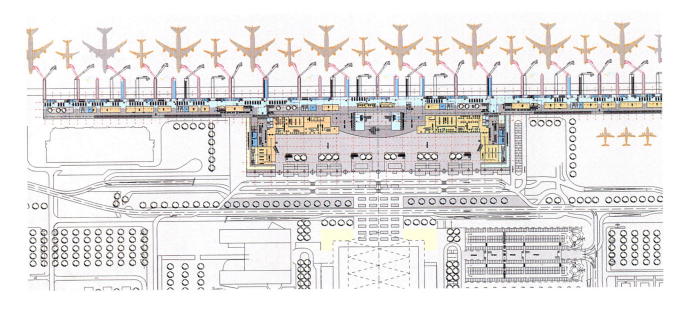

Flughafen München, Terminal 2

Modell
Grundriß Check-In
Animation Check-In-Halle

Teilschnitt
Animation Vogelperspektive

Model
Floor plan of check-in
Animation check-in hall

Section
Animation with bird's-eye view

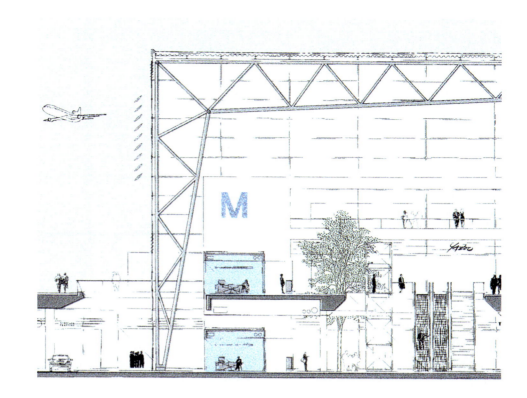

Animation Halle
Animation Halle

Im Jahre 2001 nahm J•S•K in Zusammenarbeit mit HOCH-
TIEF am Investoren- und Architektenwettbewerb für den
Ausbau des Warschauer Flughafens teil. Hier war ein stufenweise zu verwirklichendes Konzept zu entwickeln. Der Flughafen soll zunächst schrittweise bis zu einer Kapazität von
12,5 Millionen Passagieren pro Jahr und darüber hinaus erweitert werden.

Die Planungen gehen davon aus, daß nach der Realisierung
des Terminals 2 zunächst 8–10 Millionen Fluggäste pro Jahr
abgefertigt werden können. In einer zweiten Ausbaustufe sollen dann die angestrebten 12,5 Millionen erreicht werden. Ermöglicht wird diese Steigerung im Verkehrsaufkommen durch
18 Gate- und acht Vorfeldpositionen in der ersten resp. 33 Ga-
te- und 20 Vorfeldpositionen in der zweiten Ausbauphase. Im
neuen Terminal liegt die Ankunftshalle auf Ebene 02 mit
Gepäckausgabe und Zollkontrolle sowie die Check-In-Halle
auf Ebene 03 mit Abfertigungsschaltern, Warteräumen und
Sicherheitskontrolle. Für abfliegende und ankommende Reisende sind getrennte Vorfahrten geplant. Shops und Restaurants verteilen sich auf den beiden Abflugsebenen für Schen-
gen- und Non-Schengen-Passagiere. Darunter soll ein Bahnhof in das Terminal integriert werden. Auf Ebene 04 sind neben Technikflächen vor allem Büro- und Verwaltungsräume
für die Fluggesellschaften vorgesehen.

Fassaden und Dächer sollen überwiegend in Glas und Stahl
aufgelöst werden, um möglichst viel Tageslicht in die Abfertigungshalle zu bringen und das Gebäude transparent und
leicht wirken zu lassen.

*In the year 2001, in collaboration with HOCHTIEF, J•S•K
took part in an investor and architectural competition for the
development of Warsaw Airport. A concept that could be implemented in phases was required. The airport was to be enlarged step by step to achieve an initial handling capacity of
12.5 million passengers per year, with potential for further
expansion.*

*The design concept was based on the realisation of an initial
annual handling capacity of 8–10 million passengers in Terminal 2. In a second development phase the final target of
12.5 million was to be achieved. The increased traffic volume
would be handled by 18 gate and eight apron positions in the
first phase and 33 gate and 20 apron positions in the second
phase of expansion. In the new terminal the arrivals area was
located on Level 02 with the baggage claim hall and customs
as well as the check-in hall on Level 03 with check-in counters, waiting areas and security control. Separate access
roads were planned for departing and arriving passengers.
Shops and restaurants were spread out over the departures
levels for both Schengen and non-Schengen passengers. Below
this a railway station was to be integrated in the terminal. On
Level 04, in addition to rooms for technical equipment, primarily airlines administration offices and other offices were
planned.*

*Façades and roofs are mostly made of glass and steel, in or-
der to allow as much daylight as possible into the check-in
hall and to make the building appear as transparent and light
as possible.*

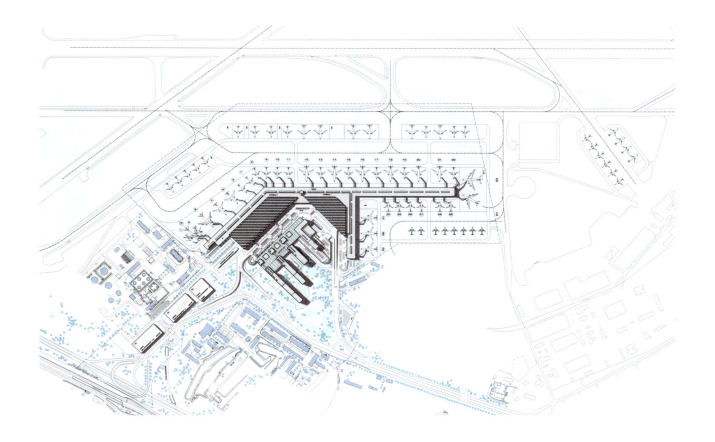

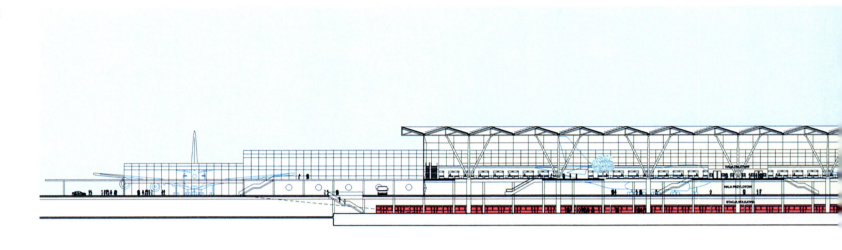

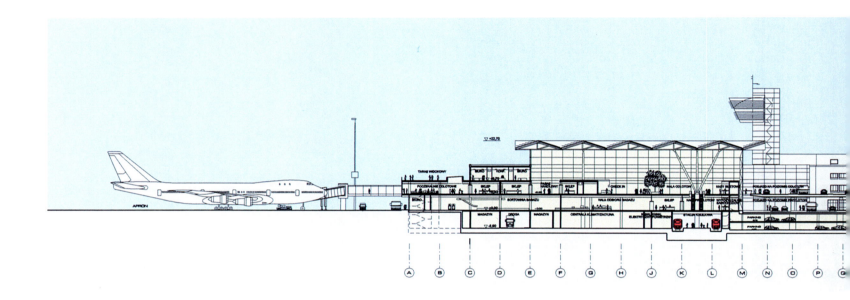

Längsschnitt Terminal
Querschnitt Terminal mit Vorfahrt
Modell Vorfeld

Animation Vorfahrt

Longitudinal section of terminal
Cross-section of terminal with access road
Model of terminal apron

Animation of access road

Flughafen Warschau, Terminal 2, Polen

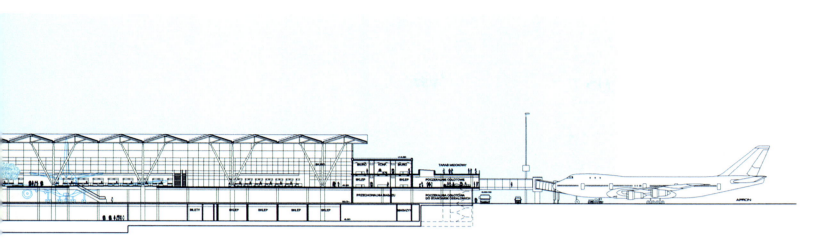

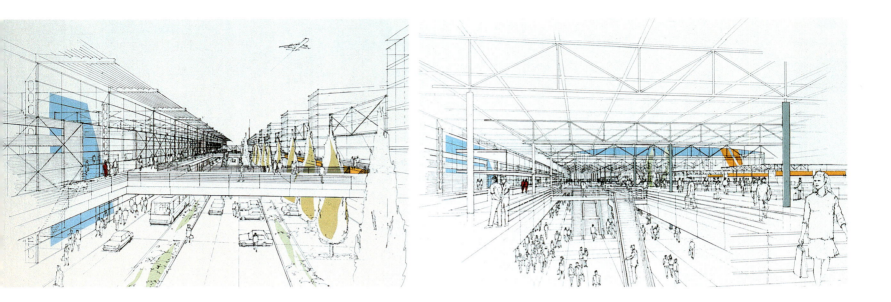

Nach der Entscheidung für Berlin als Hauptstadt des wieder-vereinigten Deutschlands wurde rasch deutlich, daß das da-mit verbundene Wachstum der Stadt nicht nur in politischer, sondern auch in wirtschaftlicher Hinsicht neue Anforderun-gen an die Quantität wie auch die Qualität des Berliner Luft-verkehrs stellen würde, denen die vorhandenen Kapazitäten nicht gewachsen waren. Das weltweit gestiegene Interesse an der Stadt und ihre zunehmende Internationalisierung ver-langten anstelle der bestehenden, kleineren in Berlin-Schöne-feld, Berlin-Tempelhof und Berlin-Tegel einen großen Flug-hafen als Drehkreuzairport. Die Standorte Tegel und Tempel-hof liegen innerhalb der Stadt und sollten zu Gunsten eines neuen Berliner Flughafens geschlossen werden.

Das erste von J•S•K in Zusammenarbeit mit der Airconsult der Frankfurt Airport Anthorty entwickelte Gutachten für Berlin untersuchte die Möglichkeiten, den Standort Schöne-feld umzuorganisieren und zu erweitern. Ein neues Terminal sollte mit dem nahegelegenen Bahnhof verbunden werden. Der Entwurf ging im ersten Schritt von 18 Millionen abzufer-tigenden Passagieren im Jahr aus und sah 40 Gate- und 18 Vorfeldpositionen sowie ein Terminal mit zwei Fingern, die senkrecht zu diesem angeordnet wurden, vor. Auf der Ebene 01 auf Vorfeld- und Vorfahrtniveau des Gebäudes soll-ten die Ankunftshalle mit Gepäckausgabe liegen und die Bus-gates zu erreichen sein. Die Abflughalle mit Check-In-Schal-tern, Sicherheitskontrolle und Warteräumen wurde auf die Ebene 02 gelegt.

Eine Passage führte zu einem Hotel- und Kongreßzentrum. Mit dem Bahnhof sollte das neue Terminal über eine quer durch eine geplante Airport City geführte Shopping-Galerie verknüpft werden. Der Entwurf zeichnet sich durch eine transparente Architektur aus.

After the decision to make Berlin the capital of a reunited Germany, it quickly became obvious that the resulting popu-lation growth in the city would also create increased demands – in terms of both quantity and quality – on Berlin's air traf-fic system, not only from a political, but also in economical point of view, which existing capacities would not be able to handle. The worldwide increase of interest in the city and its increasing globalisation made it necessary to build one major, centrally situated revolving airport to replace the existing smaller airports in the city districts of Berlin-Schönefeld, Berlin-Tempelhof and Berlin-Tegel. As Tegel and Tempelhof are located inside the city limits they were to be closed down in favour of the new Berlin Airport.

The first expert report prepared for Berlin by J•S•K, in col-laboration with Airconsult of the Frankfurt Airport Authority, investigated the possibilities of restructuring and expanding the airport in Schönefeld. A new terminal was to be connected to the nearby railway station. The concept was based on an annual handling capacity of 18 million passengers in the first phase, with 40 gate and 18 terminal apron positions, as well as a terminal with two piers in a perpendicular position to the building. Arrivals and the baggage claim hall were to be situated on Level 01 on the level of the terminal apron and the access road of the building, with direct access to the bus gates. Departures with its check-in counters, security screen-ing and waiting areas were moved to Level 02.

A walkway led to a hotel and congress centre. The new termi-nal was to be connected to the railway station via a shopping gallery running through a planned Airport City. The concept was characterised by its transparent architecture.

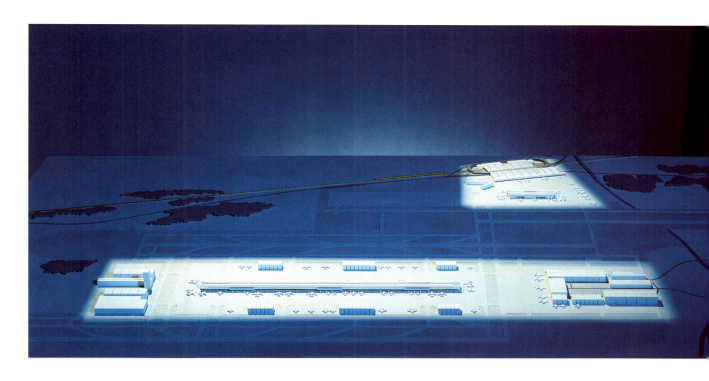

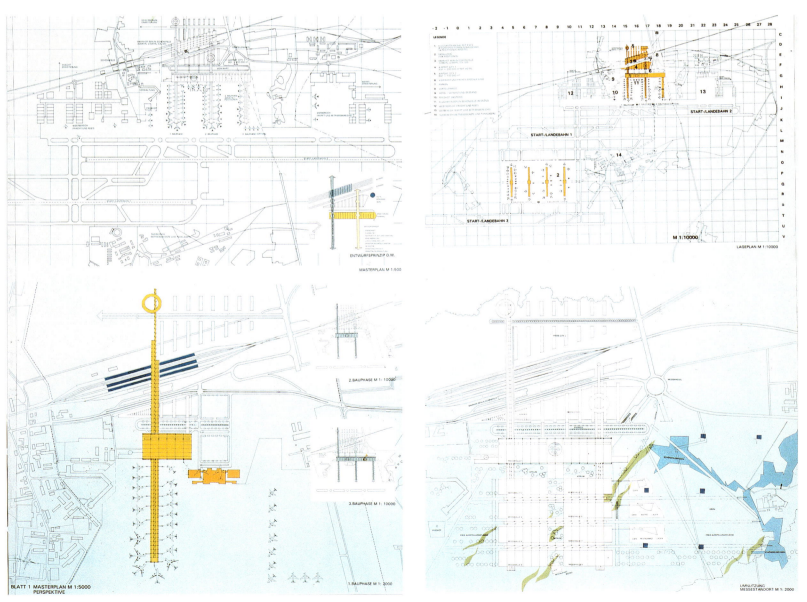

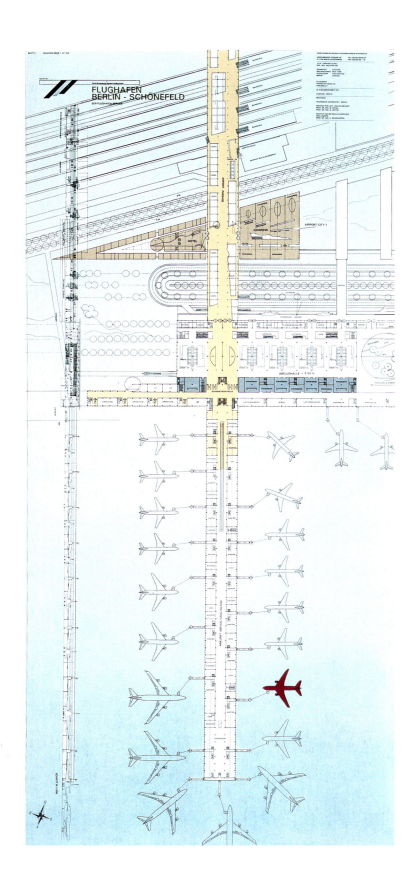

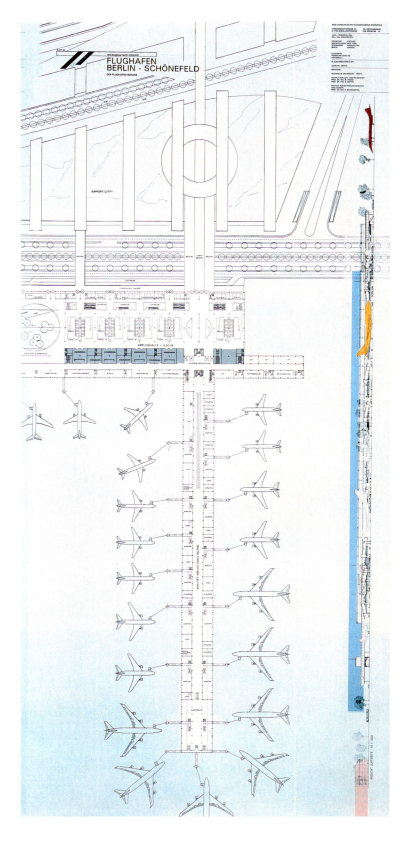

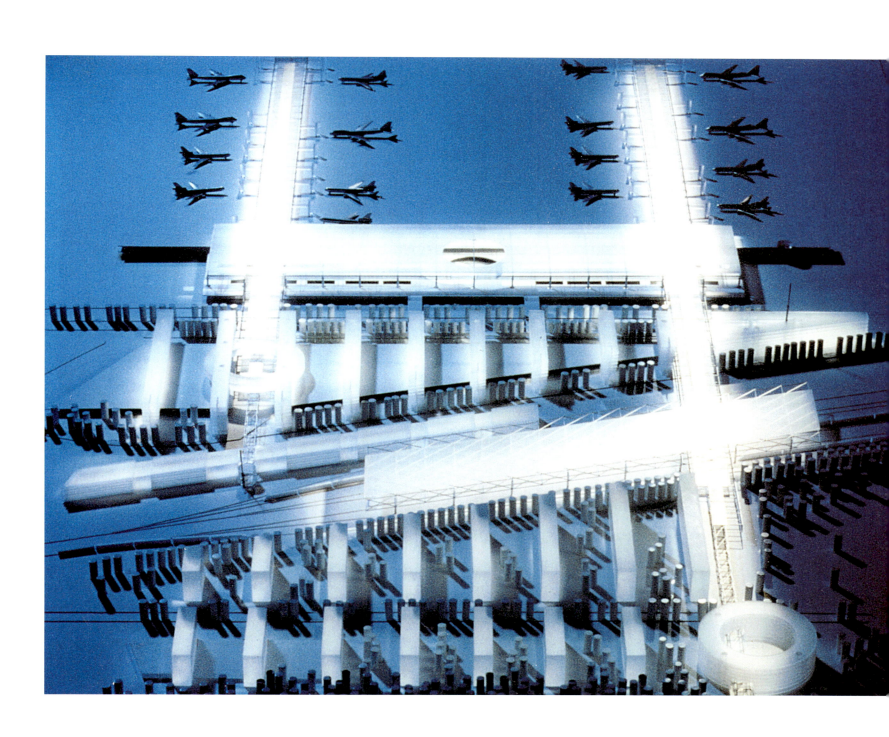

Perspektive
Perspective

In einem Gutachterverfahren sollte 1995 der geeignete Standort für einen Großflughafen Berlin untersucht werden, wobei die Ausbaumöglichkeiten zum einen in Schönefeld und zum anderen in Sperenberg auszuloten waren. Für beide Plätze erarbeitete J•S•K eine komplette Flughafenplanung, die jeweils mit der Endausbaustufe Abfertigungsmöglichkeiten für 40 Millionen Passagiere im Jahr anbieten konnte.

Die Planungen für Berlin-Schönefeld beinhalteten eine Kapazität von jährlich 23 Millionen Passagieren nach dem ersten und 30 Millionen nach dem zweiten Bauabschnitt, wobei die Gatepositionen auf 100 und schließlich 160, jene auf dem Vorfeld von 70 auf 85 zu steigern waren. Der Entwurf sah ein zentrales Abfertigungsgebäude, das direkt über dem umgestalteten Bahnhof Schönefeld lag, sowie Satelliten vor. Das Terminal hatte keine Flugzeugpositionen. Sie waren an die Satelliten angeschlossen, die zwischen zwei parallelen Startbahnen lagen, welche wiederum so angeordnet wurden, daß möglichst wenig Anwohner Störungen ausgesetzt waren. Die Satelliten der beiden ersten Bauabschnitte sollten unterirdisch durch ein Passagier-Transfer-System (PTS) erschlossen werden. Der PTS-Bahnhof wurde zusammen mit dem Bahnhof unter dem zentralen Terminal auf Ebene 01 integriert. Diese Ebene sollte ferner als Technikgeschoß dienen und Parkplätze aufnehmen. Zusätzliche Parkmöglichkeiten und eine Gepäcksortieranlage waren auf der Vorfeldebene 02 vorgesehen, auf deren Niveau auch die Bahnsteige und die Busgates geplant waren. Darüber wurde die Ankunftshalle auf Ebene 03 mit Gepäckausgabe, Autovermietung sowie Paß- und Zollkontrolle für ankommende Reisende untergebracht. Der Check-In mit Countern, Airlinebüros und Sicherheitskontrolle für abfliegende Passagiere wurde auf die Ebene 04 verlegt. Ankunft und Abflug sind an getrennte Vorfahrten und an den darunter liegenden Bahnhof angeschlossen.

Expertise proceedings were initiated in 1995 to determine the most suitable location for a major Berlin Airport, in which the potential for expansion in Schönefeld and in Sperenberg were to be evaluated and compared. J•S•K prepared concepts for complete airports at both locations, each of which would have an annual handling capacity of 40 million passengers upon completion.

The design concept for Berlin-Schönefeld allowed for an annual handling capacity of 23 million passengers after the first stage of development and 30 million after the second, whereby the number of gate areas would be increased first to 100 and then to 160, and the number of aircraft positions on the terminal apron would be increased from 70 to 85. The concept included a central passenger handling terminal, situated directly above the reconstructed Schönefeld railway station, as well as satellite terminals. The terminal had no docking positions; these were connected to the satellite terminals, which were positioned between two parallel take-off runways, in such a way as to reduce air traffic noise as much as possible for nearby residents. An underground Passenger Transfer System (PTS) would connect the satellite terminals in the first phase of construction.

The PTS terminal was to be integrated under the main terminal on Level 01, together with the railway station. This level was also to provide rooms for technical equipment and also parking facilities. Additional parking and a baggage sorting machine were planned for apron Level 02, as well as the train platforms and the bus gates. Above this were the arrivals area with the baggage claim hall on Level 03, the car rental desk as well as passport and customs check points for arriving passengers. The check-in area with its counters, airline offices and security screening for departing passengers was situated on Level 04. Arrivals and Departures would be reached by separate access roads and also connected to the railway station below.

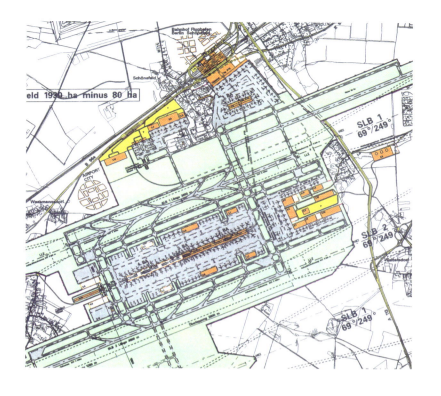

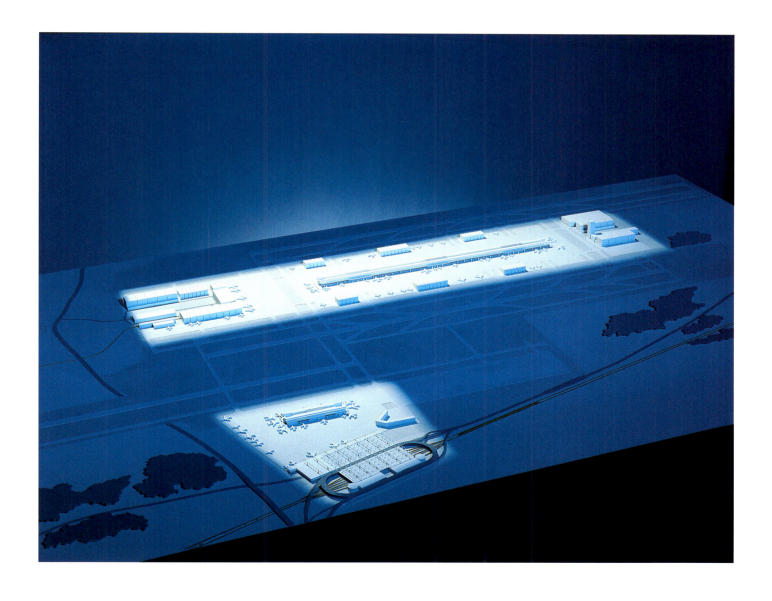

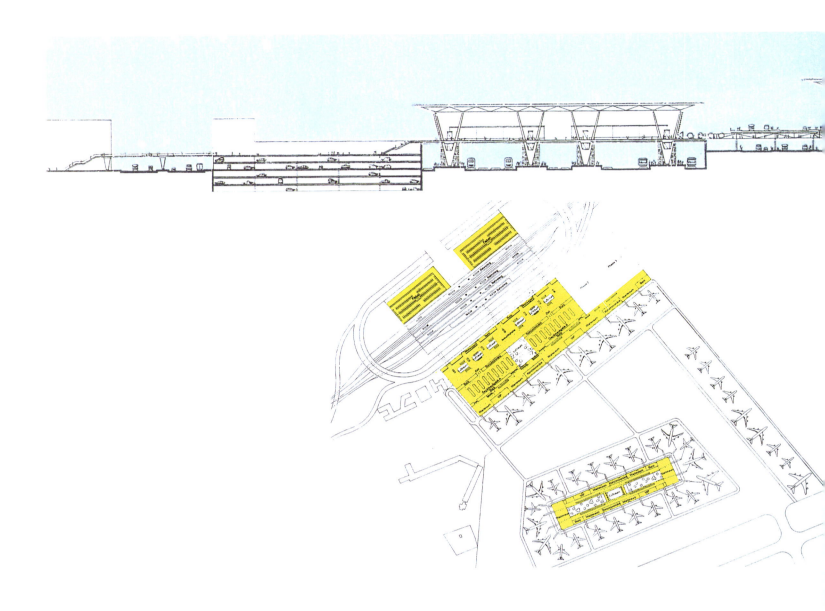

Schnitt
Ankunftsebene
Modell gesamt

Perspektive Innenraum
Modell 1. Bauabschnitt

Section
Arrivals level
Model of entire airport

Perspective of interior
Model of 1st development phase

Internationales Gutachten Flughafen Berlin / Standort Schönefeld

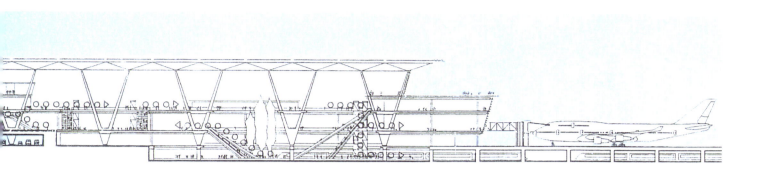

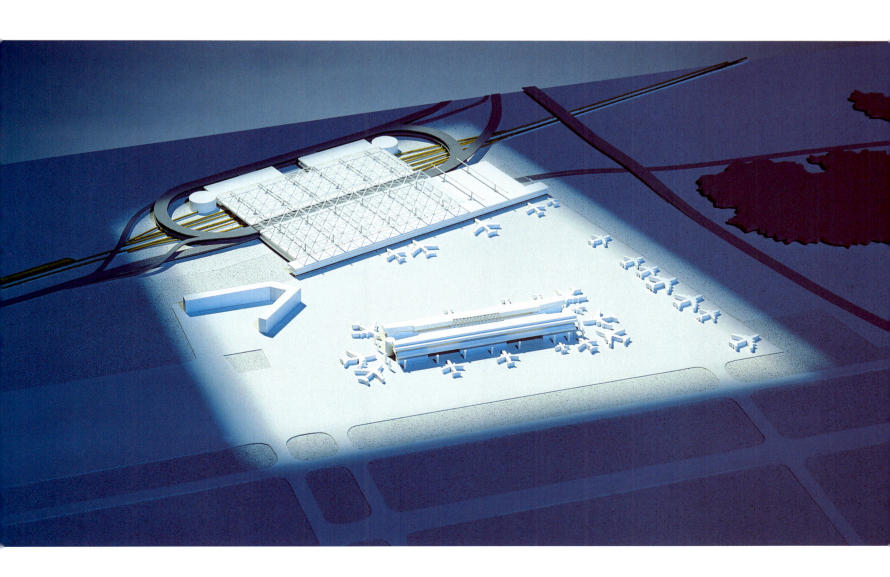

Die Entscheidung von J•S•K fiel beim bereits erwähnten Gut-achterverfahren des Jahres 1995 zunächst für den Standort Sperenberg. Er erschien für einen Großflughafen Berlin schon deshalb geeigneter zu sein als Schönefeld, weil sich hier – bei gleich guter Erreichbarkeit – erheblich weniger bebautes Gebiet in der Nähe befand und sich somit auch größere Entwicklungs-möglichkeiten boten. So war geplant, bis 2004 in Sperenberg einen Flughafen in drei Ausbaustufen mit Kapazitäten bis ca. 40 Millionen Passagieren jährlich zu schaffen, mit 120 Gate-positionen sowie 85 Vorfeldpositionen.

Das geplante Terminal im Zentrum der von J•S•K entworfenen Anlage mit seinem Y-förmigen Flugsteig, der senkrecht zum Terminal steht, erstreckt sich direkt über einem neuen Fern-bahnhof; so werden Schiene und Luft miteinander verknüpft. Die Bahnhofsebene umfaßt neben den Bahnsteigen einen dar-unter liegenden Bahnhof für das PTS.

Ebene 03, die Ankunftsebene, mit der Gepäckausgabe, Warte-räumen, Paß- und Zollkontrolle sowie die Check-In-Ebene 04 mit Countern, Airlinebüros und Sicherheitskontrolle sind über getrennte Vorfahrten erschlossen. Der Y-förmige Finger wird ergänzt durch zwei X-förmige Satelliten, die in späteren Bau-phasen realisiert werden können. Sie werden über ein PTS an die Bahnhofsebene 01 angebunden.

Das vorgeschlagene Konzept erlaubt eine hohe Flexibilität und Erweiterbarkeit.

The decision had actually been made in favour of the Speren-berg location when the above-mentioned expertise was being prepared by J•S•K in the year 1995. Sperenberg seemed more appropriate than Schönefeld as a location for building a ma-jor Berlin Airport – although both were equally accessible – because there was considerably less developed land in the vicinity and therefore greater possibilities for airport expan-sion. Thus it was planned to build an airport in three devel-opment phases in Sperenberg, to be completed by 2004, with a handling capacity of up to 40 million passengers per year, 120 gate areas and a further 85 aircraft docking positions on the apron.

The planned terminal in the centre of the J•S•K concept with its Y-shaped pier in a perpendicular arrangement to the ter-minal, is situated directly above a new railway station for long-distance trains; in this way rail and air traffic are dir-ectly linked. Besides the train platforms, the railway station level includes a terminal for the People Transfer System below. Separate access roads service Arrivals Level 03, with the bag-gage claim hall, waiting areas, passport and customs check points, and the check-in area on Level 04, with counters, air-line offices and security check points. The Y-shaped pier is supplemented by two X-shaped satellite terminals, which can be realised in later stages of development. They will be con-nected to the railway station on Level 01 by the PTS system. The proposed concept allows for a high level of flexibility and potential for expansion.

Lageplan
Modell Übersicht

Ground plan
Model of overview

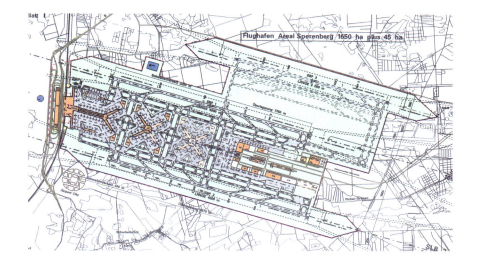

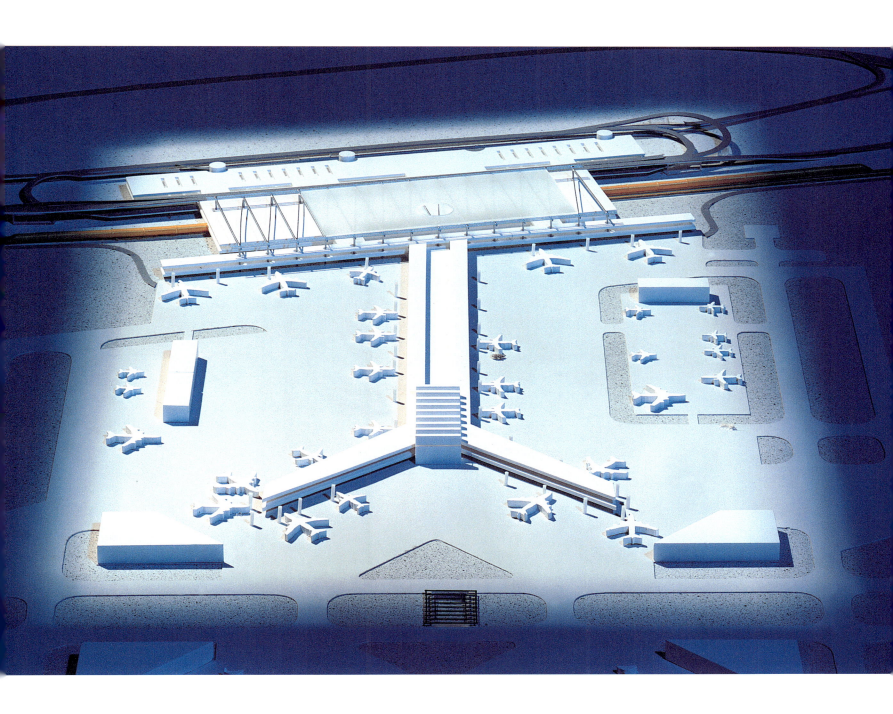

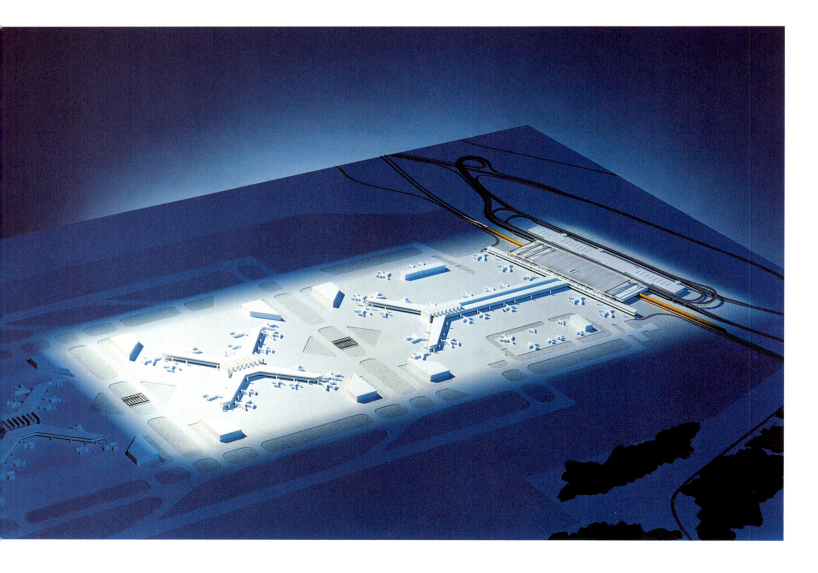

Internationales Gutachten Flughafen Berlin / Standort Speerenberg

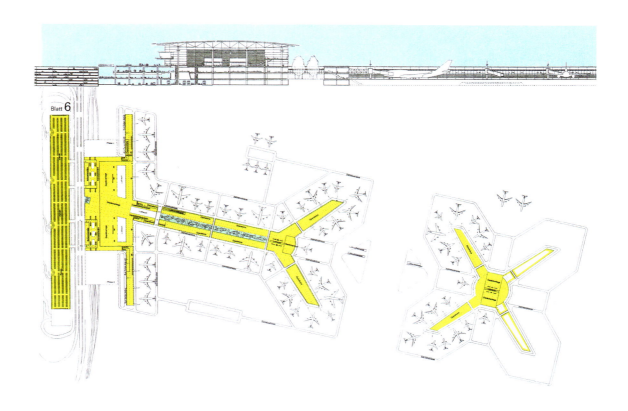

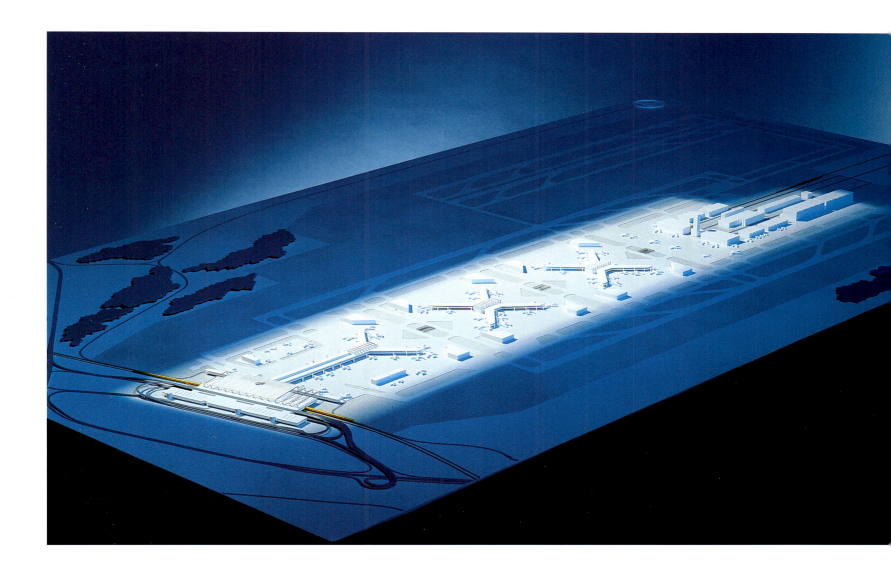

1999 fand schließlich ein kombinierter internationaler Investoren- und Architektenwettbewerb für einen bis 2007 zu realisierenden Flughafen Berlin–Brandenburg International am Standort Berlin-Schönefeld statt. J•S•K erarbeitete für die Investorengruppe IVG Pläne für eine völlig neue Flughafenanlage in sog. H-Form zwischen den parallelen Startbahnen. Zu den grundsätzlichen Überlegungen gehörte, daß ein Konzept zu entwickeln war, das auf ein PTS verzichten konnte. Die Planungen gingen außerdem weiterhin von einer jährlichen Abfertigung von zunächst 30 und in der Endausbaustufe 45 Millionen Passagieren pro Jahr aus sowie von 72 Gatepositionen am Gebäude und 58 Positionen auf dem Vorfeld bei 30 Millionen Passagieren pro Jahr.

Der projektierte Flughafen, der H-förmig angelegt wurde, besteht aus einem 700 Meter langen und 100 Meter breiten Terminal als ihrem 'Querbalken' und aus ca. 1400 Meter langen und 35 Meter breiten Pieren. Bahnhof, Ankunft, Abflug für Schengen-Reisende sowie für Non-Schengen-Passagiere sind auf vier Geschoßebenen übereinander angeordnet. Zu Ankunft und Abflug führen getrennte Vorfahrten. Sie sind auffallend lang, um den Weg zu den Check-In-Schaltern, die sich auf der Abflugsebene 03 befinden, besonders kurz zu halten. Die sich galerieartig öffnenden Ebenen, welche die diversen Nutzungen und Ausstattungen des Flughafens in Form von eingestellten Elementen aufnehmen sollen, gewähren großzügige vertikale Verbindungen zwischen den Ankunfts- und Abflugsbereichen und dem unterirdischen Bahnhof in einer ausgewogen proportionierten Halle. Der unterirdische Bahnhof bietet die Anbindung an den Fernbahnverkehr und zwei S-Bahnlinien sowie einen Flughafenexpreß für Berlin.

Die gekrümmte, alle Bauteile überspannende Dachkonstruktion verspricht, außen wie innen zum besonderen Charakteristikum des Ensembles zu werden. Dabei betont die Überhöhung in der Mittelzone die zentrale Achse, um die sich die gesamte Anlage gruppiert. Der H-förmige Grundriß ermöglicht zum einen eine sinnvolle Teilung in funktionale Einheiten und gewährleistet andererseits die erforderlichen 72 Gebäudepositionen. Die Transparenz der Fassaden und Dächer erleichtert den Reisenden die Orientierung durch zu jeder Zeit gegebene Sichtbeziehungen nach außen. Richtungsänderungen sind klar zu erkennen.

In seiner Kubatur fügt sich das Terminal mit seiner ausgesprochen eleganten Stahlkonstruktion ideal in die umgebende Landschaft ein.

In 1999 a combined international investor and architectural competition took place for a Berlin–Brandenburg International Airport, to be completed by 2007, on the site of the present Berlin-Schönefeld Airport. J•S•K prepared a concept for IVG Investorengruppe for a completely new airport system in a so-called H-form between parallel take-off runways. Part of the basic idea was to develop a concept that would work without a PTS. The concept was also based on an initial annual handling capacity of 30 million passengers, with 72 gate areas at the terminal building and 58 docking positions on the apron. This capacity would be increased to 45 million in the final phase of development.

The projected airport, designed in the shape of an 'H', consists of a terminal that is 700 metres long and 100 metres wide as a kind of 'crossbeam', with a pier that is approx. 1400 metres long and 35 metres wide. A railway station and Arrivals and Departures for Schengen and non-Schengen passengers are organised on four levels. Separate access roads lead to and from Arrivals and Departures. They are noticeably long, in order to make the distance to the check-in counters on Departures Level 03 as short as possible. The open gallery-style levels, which are to be equipped with a wide variety of airport facilities, guarantee generous vertical connections between the arrivals and departures areas and the underground railway station in a well-proportioned concourse. The underground railway station offers links to long-distance rail traffic and two commuter train lines as well as an airport express to service the city of Berlin.

The crooked roof construction, which covers all parts of the building, promises to become a special characteristic of the entire structure. Its raised middle section emphasises the central axis, around which the entire building is grouped. The H-shaped floor plan allows for a very practical division into functional units on the one hand, while accommodating the required 72 docking positions on the other. The transparency of the façades and roof makes it easier for the passengers to orientate themselves and provides a good view to the outside at all times. Changes in direction can be clearly recognised.

The cubical terminal, with its extremely elegant steel construction, fits in ideally with the surrounding landscape.

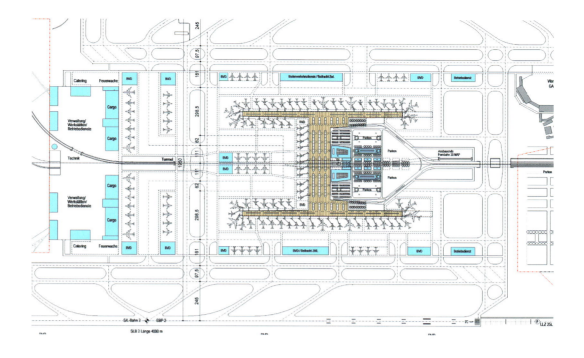

Längsschnitt
Grundriß Check-In
Animation Check-In-Halle

Animation Check-In-Halle
  mit Blick in den Bahnhof
Südpier Wartebereich

Longitudinal section
Floor plan of check-in
Animation of check-in hall

Animation check-in hall
  with view of railway station
South pier waiting area

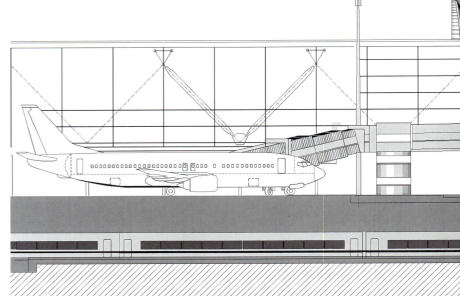

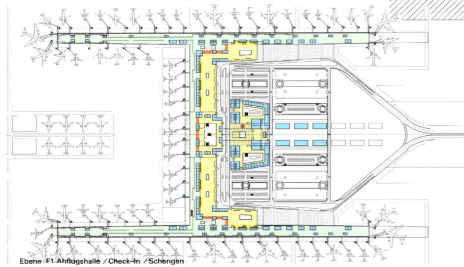

Ebene F1 Abflugshalle / Check-In / Schengen

Flughafen Berlin–Brandenburg International

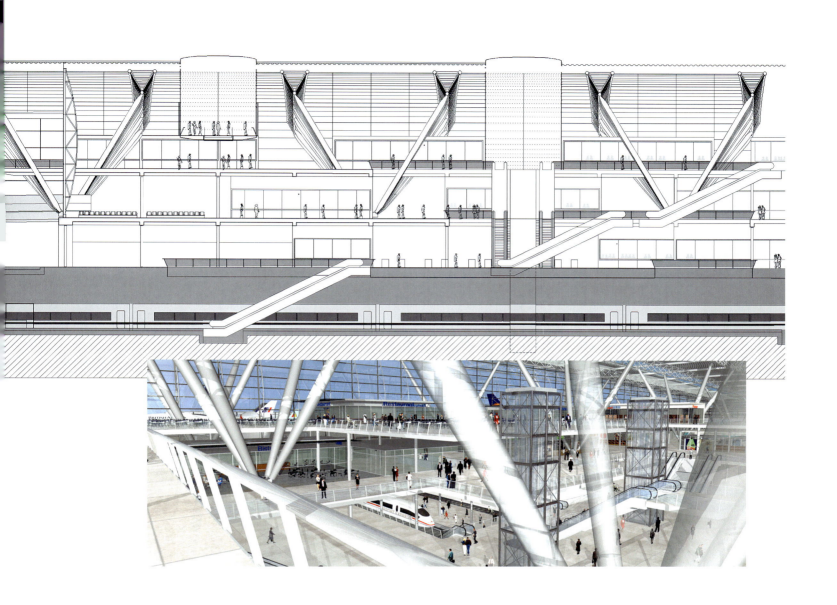

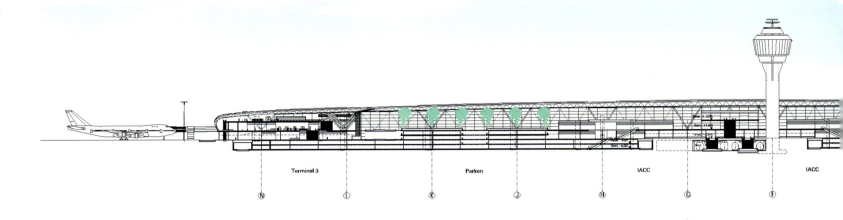

Terminal 3   Parken   IACC   IACC

Ⓝ   Ⓛ   Ⓚ   Ⓙ   Ⓗ   Ⓖ   Ⓕ

Längsschnitt
Animation Vogelperspektive Vorfahrt

Animation Vorfahrt
Modell Vorfeldseite

Longitudinal section
Animation with bird's-eye view
  of access road

Animation access road
Model of apron side

Flughafen Berlin–Brandenburg International

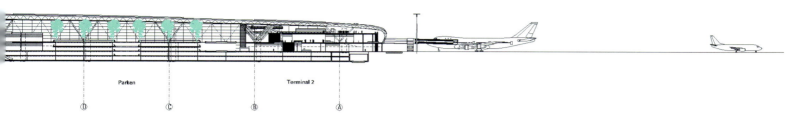

Parken   Terminal 2

Werkverzeichnis
List of Works

1991 W

Chek Lap Kok
AirportHongkong, China

1994

Terminal 2
Flughafen Frankfurt am Main

1995

Flughafen Münster-Osnabrück

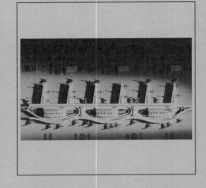

1996 W

Shanghai Pu Dong
International Airport
Shanghai, China

1994 G

Flughafen Brunei

1995 G

Flughafen Buenos Aires

1994 W

Flughafen Dublin

1995 G

Flughafen Ezeiza, Beirut

1995

Cargogebäude Flughafen Hahn

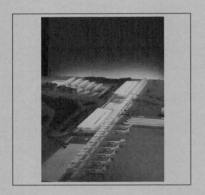

1992 W

Flughafen Köln-Bonn

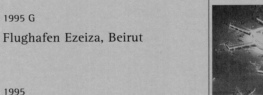

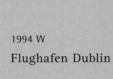

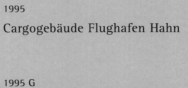

1995 G

Flughafen Malaysia

1995 G

Flughafen Stendal

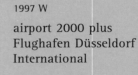

1995 G

Flughafen Berlin–Brandenburg
International
Berlin-Schönefeld

1997 W

airport 2000 plus
Flughafen Düsseldorf
International

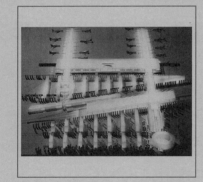

1992 G

Terminal
Flughafen Berlin-Schönefeld

1993 G

Airport Business Center
Flughafen Berlin-Schönefeld

1996

Flugsteig C
Flughafen Düsseldorf
International

1997

Cargogebäude Süd
Flughafen Frankfurt am Main

1994 G

Flughafen
Hamburg-Fuhlsbüttel

1995 G

Flughafen Berlin–Brandenburg
International, Sperenberg

1997

Flugsteig D
Flughafen Frankfurt am Main

1998

Flugsteig C
Flughafen Frankfurt am Main

1999 W

Flughafen Berlin–Brandenburg
International

2001

Zentralgebäude
Flughafen Düsseldorf
International

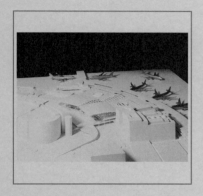

1997 G

Flughafen Zürich 2000,
Schweiz

1998 W

Terminal 2
Flughafen München

1998 G

Flughafen Saarbrücken

2000

Athens International Airport
Eleftherios Venizelos,
Griechenland

2001

Flugsteig B
Flughafen Düsseldorf
International

1998

Flugsteig A
Flughafen Düsseldorf
International

1999

Verlängerung Flugsteig A
Flughafen Frankfurt am Main

2001 (Bauantrag)

AiRail Terminal
Flughafen Frankfurt am Main

2001 W

Flughafen Warschau, Polen

2001 W

Flughafen Ramstein

2001 G

Flughafen Moskau VNUKOWO

Wettbewerbe
competitions

Platz	Real.	Jahr	Projekt
3		1991	Commerzbank AG, Frankfurt am Main
3		1991	Chek Lap Kok Airport, Hongkong
2		1992	Flughafen Köln-Bonn
2		1992	ARAG 2000, Düsseldorf
1		1992	Stadthalle mit Hotel, Düsseldorf
2		1992	Rathaus Hattersheim
Sonderankauf		1992	Parkboulevard Storkower Straße, Berlin
2		1993	Adam Opel Hochhaus, Rüsselsheim
1		1993	Alter Neckarstadtbahnhof, Mannheim
1	•	1993	CMF Congress Center Messe Frankfurt, Frankfurt am Main
3		1993	IKB Industriekreditbank, Düsseldorf
2		1993	Mercedes Benz, Düsseldorf
2		1993	Wohnheim Volkardeyer Straße, Ratingen
1	•	1994	Büro- und Geschäftshaus Frankfurter Welle, Frankfurt am Main
1	•	1994	Wohn- und Bürogebäude Mainzer Landstraße, Frankfurt am Main
2		1995	DT-Bau / Telekom, Frankfurt am Main
1		1995	Hochhaus Oberbilk, Düsseldorf
3		1996	Pu Dong International Airport, Shanghai
2	•	1996	Erweiterung HWI, Düsseldorf
1		1997	Arthouse CinemaxX, Hannover
1	•	1997	Design-Center Stilwerk, Düsseldorf
3		1997	ICE Bahnhof Limburg
3		1997	Messe Düsseldorf, NOWEA 2000
1		1997	Musical- und Entertainment-Center am Hauptbahnhof, Düsseldorf
1		1997	Reha-Klinik, Baden-Baden
1	•	1997	Flughafen Düsseldorf International, airport 2000 plus
1	•	1998	Nordostpark Nürnberg
2		1998	Flughafen München, Terminal 2
2		1998	New Global Headquarters Hoechst Marion Roussel, Frankfurt-Höchst
1	•	1998	Einkaufs- und Unterhaltungszentrum Flingern, Düsseldorf
1		1998	Umbau Rheinstadion Düsseldorf, WM 2004
1	•	1999	Technik und Innovations Park TIP, München
1	•	1999	AIRail Terminal, Flughafen Frankfurt am Main
1	•	1999	Info-Park Nord, Budapest
1		1999	Quartierzentrum Edwardsviertel, Frankfurt am Main
1		2000	Rathausdreieck Berlin-Lichtenberg
3		2000	Bürogebäude SMS Demag AG, Düsseldorf
1		2000	Spitze Speditionsstraße, Düsseldorf
1	•	2001	Rheinarena Düsseldorf
2		2001	Design-Center Stilwerk, Stuttgart
Ankauf		2002	Terminal 3, Flughafen Frankfurt am Main
Ankauf		2002	Fachhochschule Mainz
1		2002	Hochhaus GAP, Düsseldorf
1		2003	Bildungszentrum Frankfurt am Main
1		2003	Main-Kinzig-Kreisverwaltung, Gelnhausen

Anhang
Appendix

Biographien | *Biographies*
Mitarbeiter | *Collaborators*
Bürostandorte | *Office Addresses*
Veröffentlichungen | *Publications*
Fotografien, Animationen und Perspektiven |
Photographs, Animations and Perspectives

Geschäftsleitung

Helmut W. Joos

Geboren in Neuenburg / Württ.
Architekturstudium in Karlsruhe und Mainz

1961	Diplom
1962	Bürogründung in Frankfurt am Main
1970	Planungsgruppe Joos-Schulze
1980	Gründungsgesellschafter J•S•K
1981	Gesellschafter J•S•K Düsseldorf
1991	Gesellschafter J•S•K Perkins & Will International Architekten und Ingenieure GmbH
1995	Gesellschafter / Geschäftsführer J•S•K Berlin
1995	Gesellschafter J•S•K International Architekten und Ingenieure GmbH
1998	Gesellschafter J•S•K Warschau GmbH

Karsten Krüger-Heyden

Geboren in Wolfsburg
Architekturstudium in Braunschweig

1972	Diplom
1972/73	Mitarbeit im Büro Prof. F. W. Kraemer, Pfennig, Sieverts, Braunschweig
1973	Graduierten-Stipendium der TU Braunschweig
1973–79	Wissenschaftlicher Assistent am Entwurfslehrstuhl C, TU Braunschweig
1979	Partner mit R. W. Schulze in Braunschweig
1980	Gründungsgesellschafter J•S•K
1991–95	Geschäftsführer J•S•K Perkins & Will International Architekten und Ingenieure GmbH
1995–98	Gesellschafter J•S•K International Architekten und Ingenieure GmbH
1995–98	Gesellschafter J•S•K Berlin

Jurek M. Slapa

Geboren in Königshütte / Ob.schl.
Architekturstudium in Krakau und Aachen

1966–69	Studienreise mit Büropraktika in Wien, Mailand und Budapest
1970	Diplom
1970–87	Mitarbeit HPP Architekten, Düsseldorf
1988	Gesellschafter J•S•K Düsseldorf
1989	Gesellschafter J•S•K Frankfurt am Main

Helmut Oberholz

Geboren in Heiligenhaus
Architekturstudium in Essen

1976	Diplom

Architekturstudium in Berlin und Aachen

1981	Diplom
1977–87	Mitarbeit im Architekturbüro Motes, Heiligenhaus
1988	Partner J•S•K Düsseldorf
1990	Gesellschafter J•S•K Düsseldorf
1992	Gesellschafter J•S•K Frankfurt am Main

Zbigniew M. Pszczulny

Geboren in Thorn
Architekturstudium in Danzig

1976	Diplom
1976–80	Mitarbeit bei Miastoprojekt, Thorn
1980/81	Europäische Studienreise
1981–88	Mitarbeit HPP Architekten, Düsseldorf
1988	Partner J•S•K Düsseldorf
1990	Gesellschafter J•S•K Düsseldorf
1991	Gesellschafter J•S•K Frankfurt am Main
1995–98	Gesellschafter J•S•K Berlin
1998	Gesellschafter J•S•K Warschau GmbH

Gunter P. J. Bürk

Geboren in Schwenningen a. N.
Architekturstudium in Stuttgart

1967	Diplom
1968	Aufbaustudium Städtebautechnik in Mainz
1969	Mitarbeit Perkins & Will Architects Washington, D. C., USA
1980	Partner Perkins & Will Architects
1983	Senior Partner Perkins & Will Architects
1988	Gastdozent Catholic University of America, Washington, D. C., USA
1991	Geschäftsführer J•S•K Perkins & Will International Architekten und Ingenieure GmbH
1992	Gesellschafter J•S•K Frankfurt am Main
1995	Gesellschafter J•S•K Berlin
1995	Gesellschafter / Geschäftsführer J•S•K International Architekten und Ingenieure GmbH

Planung

Ulrich Bönsel

Geboren in Lanzenhain / Hessen
Bauingenieurstudium in Gießen
1981   Diplom
1981   Mitarbeit im Büro J•S•K
       Frankfurt am Main
1990   Gesellschafter J•S•K
       Frankfurt am Main

Michael Stutz

Geboren in Düsseldorf
Architekturstudium in Darmstadt und Aachen
1987   Diplom
1988–90   Mitarbeit Perkins & Will Architects
       Chicago, Illinois, USA
1990/91   Mitarbeit Murphy & Jahn, Chicago
       Illinois, USA
1991/92   Mitarbeit Suter & Suter AG,
       Zürich, Schweiz
1992   Mitarbeit J•S•K Berlin
1995   Gesellschafter J•S•K Berlin

Wolfgang Marcour

Geboren in Bergisch Gladbach
Architekturstudium in Aachen
1990   Diplom
1990   Mitarbeit J•S•K Düsseldorf
1999   Gesellschafter J•S•K Düsseldorf

Joachim Lepper

Geboren in Hohenlimburg / Westf.
Architektur- und Städtebaustudium in
       Braunschweig
1972   Diplom
       Wirtschaftswissenschaftliches
       Aufbaustudium in Braunschweig
1970–78   Mitarbeit im Büro Joos-Schulze,
       Frankfurt / Braunschweig
1978   Gründung Büro für Architektur
       und Stadtplanung in Braunschweig
1985   Lehrauftrag / Seminar an der
       TU Braunschweig
1997   Wohnungsbauseminar
       TU Braunschweig
1997   Städtebauseminar TU Braunschweig
Seit 2003   Gesellschafter J•S•K International
       Architekten und Ingenieure GmbH

Eberhard Weber

Geboren in Leutershausen / Bayern
Bauingenieurstudium in Nürnberg
1962   Diplom
1964–66   Architekt bei GSG
       Frankfurt am Main
1966   Mitarbeit bei Helmut W. Joos,
       Frankfurt am Main
1990   Gesellschafter J•S•K
       Frankfurt am Main

Jonas J. Jacobitz

Geboren in Biesenthal / Brandenburg
Architekturstudium in Darmstadt und
Düsseldorf
1974   Diplom
1974–76   Mitarbeit bei Prof. Eller, Moser,
       Walter, Düsseldorf
1976–84   Mitarbeit im Architekturbüro
       Olaf Jacobsen, Düsseldorf
1984–89   Mitarbeit HPP Architekten,
       Düsseldorf
1989   Mitarbeit J•S•K Düsseldorf
1992   Partner J•S•K Frankfurt am Main
1999   Gesellschafter J•S•K Düsseldorf

Mariusz Rutz

Geboren in Thorn
Architekturstudium in Danzig und München
1985–91   Studienreise mit Büropraktika in
       Basel und München
1991   Examen
1991–94   Mitarbeit HENN Architekten
       Ingenieure, München
1994–96   Eigenes Büro in Berlin
1996   Mitarbeit J•S•K
       Berlin / Düsseldorf
1998   Mitarbeit J•S•K Architekten
       Warschau GmbH
2000   Gesellschafter J•S•K Architekten
       Warschau GmbH

William R. Joslin

Geboren in Dante, Virginia, USA
1981   Bachelor of Design in Architecture,
       University of Florida, USA
1982–85   Mitarbeit bei BKS und ADG
       Architects in Orlando, Florida, USA
1987   Master of Architecture, University
       of Illinois at Chicago, USA
1986–95   Mitarbeit Perkins & Will Architects
       Chicago, Illinois, USA
1989–91   Mitarbeit Perkins & Will Architects
       London, England
1991   Mitarbeit J•S•K Frankfurt am Main
       und Berlin
1995   Gesellschafter J•S•K Berlin

Florian Beck

Geboren in Sigmaringen
1987   Universität Stuttgart
       Architektur und Städtebau
1992–93   Illinois Institute of Technology
       Chicago, Illinois, USA
       IIT International Scholarship
1994   Diplom
1995–96   Harvard University Graduate
       School of Design Camprige, USA
       Rotary Foundation Stipendium
1992–97   Mitarbeit in Architekturbüros in
       Stuttgart, Berlin, Graz und Chicago
1997   Mitarbeit J•S•K Berlin
2000   Gesellschafter J•S•K Berlin

Lothar Simonis

Geboren in Wiesbaden
Architekturstudium in Wiesbaden
1980   Diplom
1980–82   Mitarbeit bei Vesterling, Wiesbaden
1983–90   Mitarbeit bei Rühle, Sindelfingen
1991–93   Mitarbeit bei Vesterling, Wiesbaden
1994–96   Mitarbeit bei Jo Franzke,
       Frankfurt am Main
1997   Mitarbeit bei
       KSP Engel + Zimmermann,
       Frankfurt am Main
1998   Mitarbeit J•S•K Düsseldorf
2002   Gesellschafter J•S•K Düsseldorf

Bauleitung

Karl-Peter Peters

Geboren in Berlin-Tempelhof
Architekturstudium in Idstein i. Ts.
1969	Diplom
1969	Mitarbeit bei Helmut W. Joos, Frankfurt am Main
1988	Gesellschafter J•S•K Frankfurt am Main

Manfred Stauss

Geboren in Eisenhausen, Krs. Marburg
Bauingenieurstudium in Siegen
1986	Diplom
1986–95	Mitarbeit J•S•K Frankfurt am Main
1995	Gesellschafter J•S•K Frankfurt am Main

Frank Schütz

Geboren in Marienberg i. Westerwald
Bauingenieurstudium in Idstein i. Ts.
1984	Diplom
1984	Mitarbeit J•S•K Frankfurt am Main
1989	Gesellschafter J•S•K Frankfurt am Main

Volker Rumler

Geboren in Wilden, Krs. Siegen
Bauingenieurstudium in Siegen
1979	Diplom
1979–82	Mitarbeit im Statikbüro Lüthke, Siegen
1982–84	Mitarbeit Ph. Holzmann AG, Frankfurt, Auslandsabteilung Mittlerer Osten
1984–87	Auslandseinsatz Ph. Holzmann AG, Saudi-Arabien
1987–89	Werksleiter IMBAU Fertigteilwerk, Rinteln
1989/90	Mitarbeit Ph. Holzmann AG, Frankfurt, Auslandsabteilung Europa
1990	Mitarbeit J•S•K Frankfurt am Main
1995	Gesellschafter J•S•K Berlin

Mitarbeiter
Collaborators

Jasmin Ankenbrand
Thorsten Augustin
Peter Otto Bambach
Jeanette Bauch
Hannelore Beatty
Florian Beck
Heike Biechteler
Johannes Blank
Ulrich Bönsel
Danilo Bogdanovic
Luise Bormann
Bettina Boyens
Yvonne Brandenburger
Lothar Brunk
Christian Büdel
Gunter Bürk
Nicola Bürk
Gerhard Burg
Dan-Peter Contiu
Michael Cornelsen
Anne Crone
Krystian Czamberg
Wolfgang Dehner
Nicole Diewald
Rainer Dittmer
Joachim Dunkel
Bernd Ebeling
Andreas Edrich
Uwe Eiffert
Frank Engeler
Dietmar Eufinger-Damm
Joachim Facklam
Dirk Faltin
Michael Felka
Helga Fischer
Dietlind Frahm
Christina Frick
Simone Frings
Monika Gerharz
Georg Germroth
Jacek Golesny
Frank Gonzalez
Harro Greger
Markus Gries
Vivien Groeger
Michael Habicht
Katia von Häfen
Axel Hatzsch
Natalie Heger
Christian Heikamp
Manuela Heikamp
Wolfgang-Friedrich Heine
Juliane Heinrich
Markus Henze
Veronika Herbst
Patricia Heuser
Thomas Heuser
Sven Hiller

Annette Hoheisel
Manfred Hövel
Jonas Jacobitz
Hans-Ulrich John
Alexander Joos
Andrea Joos
Gisela Joos
Helmut Joos
Matthias Jopp
William Joslin
Daniela Jovanova
Guido Kall
Nikiforos Kappos
Wolfgang Kempe
Lars Kernler
Michael Kirchner
Peter Klein
Jascha Klusen
Heidemarie Knippel
Peter Knöbel
Andreas Knoblauch
Ursula Koeker
Daniel Kohlmeyer
Marie Luise Kolla
Jürgen Kowald
Hans Krahl
Elfrun Krämer
Karsten Krüger-Heyden
Eckhard Ksionsek
Ingrid Latz
Volker Lau
Christine Lenz
Joachim Lepper
Lothar Lesche
Mek Limmer
Markus Lücker
Lothar Lühr
Undine Lunow
Eva Luthardt
Wolfgang Marcour
Christoph Matern
Martin Menacher
Stephan Mende
Susann Metallinos
Wolfgang Metzger
Thomas Möllmann
Sandi Morese
Lutz Müller
Antonia Müller-Wallerich
Marco Nonnenmacher
Michael Numrich
Helmut Oberholz
Petra Ortmanns
Frank Ostrowski
Waldemar Ott
Bela Payer
Petra Pförtner
Karl-Peter Peters

Wolfgang Philipp
Heinrich Pieper
Roberto Poropat
Zbigniew Pszczulny
Michael Pülz
Georg Rack
Jessica Repp
Volker Rumler
Mariusz Rutz
Stefan Sahl
Aleksander Sajdak
Angelika Sallwey
Sigrid Schäfer
Klaus-Dieter Scheffel
Edith Schewerda
Monika Schiebelhut
Volker Schleyer
Silke Schmitt
Reni Schröder
Frank Schütz
Christine Schulz
Klaudia Schumacher
Ute Schuster
Renate Schwarz
Günter Schweitzer
Sabine Seelbach
Lothar Simonis
Danijela Simovic
Jurek Slapa
Jochen Solbach
Manfred Stauss
Anke Steckenreiter
Stefanie Stefanowski
Katrin Stemmann
Frank Stenger
Michael Stock
Marc Ströder
Heidrun Struckmeier
Michael Stutz
Brigitte Sutter
Lukas Sykora
Eva Tauer
Franz-Josef Thesing
Dirk Trosdorf
Gabriele Trost
Milorad Vasovic
Stefanie Wagler
Gert Warmuth
Eberhard Weber
Birgit Weinland
Oliver Weiß
Regina Winzer
Adam Zaporowski
Stefan Zwilfmeyer

Bürostandorte
Office Addresses

J•S•K Dipl. Ing. Architekten
Frankfurt am Main

Hainer Weg 50
60599 Frankfurt am Main

J•S•K Dipl. Ing. Architekten
Braunschweig

Wolfenbütteler Straße 45
38124 Braunschweig

J•S•K Dipl. Ing. Architekten
Düsseldorf

Schanzenstraße 80
40549 Düsseldorf

J•S•K Dipl. Ing. Architekten
Berlin

Marktstraße 8
10317 Berlin

J•S•K Dipl. Ing. Architekten
Baden-Baden

Mauerbergstraße 21
76534 Baden-Baden

J•S•K International
Architekten und Ingenieure GmbH

Hainer Weg 50
60599 Frankfurt am Main

J•S•K Architekci Sp. z o. o.
Warschau

ul. Kubickiego 9
PL 02-954 Warszawa

Joos & Fennel Design AG
Zürich

Südstraße 99
CH-8008 Zürich-Seefeld

1991
Ausstellung und Katalog „4ᵉ Salon International de l'Architecture", Milano, Palazzo dell'Arte
Wolkenkratzer – Die schönsten Bauten, ihre Geschichte, ihre Architektur, Hrsg. Christine Proske, Wilhelm Heyne Verlag

1992
Planungskulturen, Hrsg. Martin Wentz, Campus-Verlag
Architekturszene Deutschland, VVV-Verlag

1993
Archigrad – Planen und Bauen am 50. Breitengrad, Nr. 3 (CMF Frankfurt am Main), Verlag AFW Klaus Winkler

1994
Archigrad – Planen und Bauen am 50. Breitengrad, Nr. 4 (CMF Frankfurt; Frankfurter Welle; Gallus-Park Frankfurt), Verlag AFW Klaus Winkler
Architekten in Hessen, Verlag Buch und Film
Katalog zur Ausstellung „Lichtenberger Linie LiLi – Lichtenberg plant und baut 1991–1994, Bezirksamt Lichtenberg von Berlin

1995
Archigrad – Planen und Bauen am 50. Breitengrad, Nr. 5 (Flughafen Frankfurt am Main), Verlag AFW Klaus Winkler
Bauen und Wohnen in Berlin, Wirtschaftsverlag

1996
Stadtentwicklung, Hrsg. Martin Wentz, Campus-Verlag
Katalog zur Ausstellung „Neue Berliner Stadtquartiere", Deutsches Architektur-Museum Frankfurt am Main
Archigrad – Planen und Bauen am 50. Breitengrad, Nr. 6 (Flughafen Düsseldorf; Flughafen Münster Osnabrück), Verlag AFW Klaus Winkler
Große Architekturbüros in Deutschland, Communitas
Berlin – Visionen werden Realität, Hrsg. Christel Kapitzki, Jovis-Verlag

1997
Architekturführer Berlin, Reimer Verlag
Neue Architektur Berlin 1990–2000, Jovis Verlag

1998
Katalog zur Ausstellung „Maßstabssprung – Die Zukunft von Frankfurt am Main", Deutsches Architektur-Museum Frankfurt am Main
DBZ Deutsche Bauzeitschrift, Dienstleistungszentrum Ostkreuz Berlin, 5/1998
Neuer Wohnungsbau, Campus Verlag
Neue Bahnhöfe in Berlin, Hrsg. Christel Kapitzki, Jovis-Verlag
Berlins unbekannte Kulturdenkmäler, L & H Verlag
Berlin – Standorte für Entscheidungen, Hrsg. Senatsverwaltung für Wirtschaft und Betriebe Berlin

1999
Standort Berlin-Ostkreuz: Historische Knorr-Bremse – Industriekomplex im Wandel, Hrsg. Helmut Engel, Jovis Verlag
AW Architektur + Wettbewerbe, Neuer Städtebau – Bahnhöfe, Plätze, Wohn- und Gewerbegebiete, Karl Krämer Verlag
Berlin: Offene Stadt Bd. 1: Die Stadt als Ausstellung, Hrsg. Berliner Festspiele und Architektenkammer Berlin
Bundeshauptstadt Berlin – Wo regiert und residiert wird, Hrsg. Ulf Meyer, Jovis Verlag

2000
Gebaute Transparenz, J•S•K Architekten, Ernst Wasmuth Verlag
Architekten in Hessen, Bauten und Projekte, Verlag Buch + Film P. Diemer

2001
Standort Berlin-Marzahn: Historische Knorr-Bremse – Industriekomplex im Wandel, Hrsg. Helmut Engel, Jovis Verlag
AirPorts, J•S•K Architekten, Ernst Wasmuth Verlag

2002
Ausstellung „Passenger Terminal EXPO 2002", Hamburg

Weitere Veröffentlichungen in verschiedenen Fachzeitschriften

Fotografien, Animationen und Perspektiven
Photographs, Animations and Perspectives